Dictionary
of
Mythology

LAUREL

"THIS IS A USEFUL AND MOST UNORTHO-
DOX SELECTION."

—Leo Rosten

BERGEN EVANS

DICTIONARY OF
MYTHOLOGY

"We will not find scientific or historical truth in
mythology. But we will find poetic truth. And poetic truth may be all the truth that men will ever
know."

—From the Author's Foreword

THE LEGENDS OF GREECE AND ROME,
NORSE MYTHOLOGY, THE ARTHURIAN
LEGENDS, AND THE BEST-KNOWN FIG-
URES FROM EGYPTIAN AND BABYLONIAN
MYTHOLOGY—ALL IN READABLE, ALPHA-
BETICALLY ARRANGED ENTRIES, WITH
HELPFUL CROSS-REFERENCING

Dictionary

of

Mythology

Mainly Classical

Bergen Evans

A LAUREL BOOK
Published by
Dell Publishing
a division of
Bantam Doubleday Dell Publishing Group, Inc.
1540 Broadway
New York, New York 10036

ISBN: 0-440-20848-3

Reprinted by arrangement with Centennial Press

Printed in the United States of America

Published simultaneously in Canada

April 1991

10 9 8 7 6 5 4

OPM

FOREWORD

Myths are many things. They may be distortions of actual events. One of the least credible of the Greek myths is the story of the Minotaur, a monster half-man and half-bull, which devoured the young men and women which the Athenians were compelled to send as his victims each year. But archaeologists have dug up the great palace on Crete, which was indeed a labyrinth, and found frescoes on the walls depicting bull fights in which male and female toreadors were sent unarmed into the ring. The bull was only a bull and did not eat his assailants. But he undoubtedly gored many of them.

Myths may be fragments of dead religions. Or they may be merely personifications of philosophical or abstract ideas. Thus Salus (meaning "health") was the Roman goddess of health and Suadela (meaning "persuasion") was the goddess of persuasion, an attendant of the goddess of love. Many myths are attempts to explain seemingly meaningless customs or puzzling place names. The story of Helles was probably invented to explain the word *Hellespont* and Icarus may have come into being and taken his fatal plunge for no other reason than to give "meaning" to the Icarian Sea.

Many myths can be regarded as primitive science, expla-

FOREWORD

nations of what things "really" are and how they came to be. Thus the biblical story of the Tower of Babel explains why men speak different languages and the story of Noah explains the rainbow and used to explain why Negroes were slaves. In Greek mythology the story of Phaëthon accounted for the desolation of the Sahara and in Norse mythology Thor's enormous drinking in the hall of Utgard-Loki accounted for the tides.

Not that genuine mythology was ever deliberately invented. The genesis of a myth is slow and unconscious. Myths grow into acceptance as indisputable facts through scores of generations of telling and retelling. And in the course of such tellings new gods come into being, heroes are exalted to demigods or goddesses diminished to queens. Assuming one function, a god or a goddess was often translated into a related function. Thus Artemis, originally a goddess of childbirth, became for obvious reasons goddess of the moon and possibly because so many small animals are nocturnal she became the protectress of small creatures and of unborn young. As goddess of the moon she was twin sister to Apollo, the sun god, and sometimes syncretized with Hecate, that sinister goddess of the night. Just how Artemis became the virgin goddess of the chase is not clear—possibly because of the solitary wandering of the moon or possibly because of her overlordship of animals.

In the stories of almost any major figure in mythology there are infinite variations, duplications, contradictions, and inconsistencies. Those of us who as children read the *Tanglewood Tales* had a delightful introduction to classical mythology but a misleading one. Because Hawthorne had tidied it up too much, made it all too reasonable. So that when in our later reading we find Bellerophon and Theseus performing the same feats, when we find Hyperion sometimes the sun and sometimes the sun's father, when we find Achilles killed by Paris and Achilles killed by Apollo, when we find Iasion killed, in Homer, by one of Zeus' thunderbolts but living, in Ovid, to old age—when we find these and hundreds of other inconsistencies, we are bewildered and only gradually come to realize that the stories are far older and perhaps far more significant than Hawthorne's versions might have led us to believe.

No one patronizes mythology any more, dismissing it as "history seen through the eyes of children." Max Müller's allusion to Demeter's absentmindedly eating Pelops' shoulder as "silly, senseless and savage" seems naive to us. We simply feel that there is something in the story that we don't understand. It may once have had a meaning that got lost in confused mistellings. Or some forgotten custom is involved. Or there is something in the worship of Demeter (one of the most mysterious of the goddesses) or something in the nature of Pelops that has faded into the dark rearward and abyss of time.

A curious explanation of classical mythology was that the stories were distortions of the Scriptures. Thus Ladon, the dragon that guarded the apples of the Hesperides, was actually the serpent of the Garden of Eden. Deucalion was Noah; Hercules, Samson; Arion, Jonah; etc. This theory had an extraordinarily long life; it was espoused by Sir Walter Raleigh in the early seventeenth century and by W. E. Gladstone in the late nineteenth.

Presumably there was a time when each myth was regarded by narrator and hearer as a simple statement of fact: Aphrodite *had* risen from the sea-foam; whoso looked on Medusa *did* turn to stone; Hercules *had* dragged Cerberus up from the underworld into the light of day; the dwarfs *had* woven the magic skein by which the Fenriswolf was bound;

and Heimdal *could* hear the wool growing on the sheep in the world below him.

Some find such credulity hard to believe, not merely because the events it accepted are improbable but because accounts of them vary so. But neither of these doubts carries much weight. The whole point of the stories was that heroes and gods are not as common men, and the collection of variants is the work of modern scholarship. Most of the early believers probably knew only the one local version of a given myth and that, to them, was the true account. Our own sacred writings are full of contradictions yet few believers, even those who search the Scriptures diligently, seem to be concerned about them or even aware of them.

Mythology in antiquity was not an old wives' tale or an amusing fantasy. The stories were real and important. The farmer assumed that the growth of his crops depended upon the goodwill of Demeter or Ceres. The sailor knew that his safe return depended upon Poseidon. The pregnant woman put her faith and hope in Hero or Lucina. The supernatural was everywhere; the sea, the sky, the groves, plains, valleys and mountains, and even the underworld, were populated by invisible creatures by whose will or whim all human affairs were affected.

The human forms of the Greek deities must have comforted their worshippers with the sense—however misleading—that the cosmos was bascially human. There were dreadful monsters, to be sure, the Hecatoncheires, Phorcys, the Gorgons, Typhon, dragons, Centaurs, brazen bulls, Harpies, and so on. But the worst of these antedated the Olympians; they came from the world which the Olympians had opposed and overthrown. And in the contests between these unhuman creatures and the gods, or even the demigods or the great heroes, the mosters were almost always worsted.

So that the Olympians stood as a defensive bulwark between man and the terrible, inhuman aspects of life. Just as the Norse gods stood between man and the inhuman Frost Giants—at least until Ragnarok. Tyrannical and cruel, lustful and deceitful the gods might be, but they preserved a human order.

The Norse gods had the melancholy grandeur of being doomed. At the last great battle they would all be destroyed. And even the Greek gods were not omnipotent or eternal. Of the two doves that Zeus sent everyday to bring his ambrosia, one was always crushed by the Wandering Rocks. And there is that dismal cry, in Plutarch's *Moralia*, "full of spirit's melancholy and eternity's despair," when the wild voice called to Tammuz, the steersman, that "Great Pan is dead!" and "all the air was filled with wailing and lamentation." The frightened soothsayers at Tiberius' court said it wasn't the god that had died but a daemon of the same name. But we know better. We know now that the gods, too, die and that the Immortals are as mortal as their creators.

Myths are certainly folk history. But they are also folk poetry and no other body of literature so stimulates our imagination. They allegorize the known and start us wondering wildly about the unknown.

Some of it is prosaic, even funny: Ariadne deserted by Theseus finds solace with Bacchus; the women of Lemnos neglect the rites of Aphrodite and are punished by being given a disgusting smell; the nymph Echo chatters so persistently that Hera, exasperated, forbids her to speak anything more than the last syllable of the previous speaker. Ocnos (surely a teacher in some graduate school) forever weaves a rope of straw which an ass forever devours.

But most of it is solemn and sublime: Cronus (Time) devours his children; Poseidon, god of the sea, is violent,

FOREWORD

vengeful, and monster-producing; Pan, the god of the animal in man, fills men suddenly with overmastering fears which sweep courage and prudence—indeed, our very humanity—aside like chaff. Aphrodite, beauty, arises in "the rainbow of the salt-sand wave"; while Athena, wisdom, springs fully armed from the forehead of Zeus. For millennia men have perceived that the story of Oedipus—from his confrontation with the Sphinx to his final self-destruction—is a summation of life.

Any story that is told and retold for centuries must touch upon something common in human experience or aspiration. And that it speaks in allegory or parable rather than in direct statement enhances its effectiveness. For it moves the listener to imaginative creation.

Jack the Giant Killer, for instance, appeals to every boy's feeling that he is not appreciated and that some day those who now scorn him will see him as the clever fellow he really is. And deeper in the story is the Oedipal situation: the father —not so much transformed to as revealed as—an ogre, is outwitted and slain and Jack lives happily ever after with his mother.

Cinderella, similarly, projects the self-pity and resentment of the "unloved" girl. She—her beauty hidden under ashes—is compelled to drudge, while her ugly, hateful older sisters have all the fun and meet Prince Charming, who if he could only see Cinderella in her true loveliness would scorn the sisters and fling himself at her feet.

The greatest of modern myths, one still in the making, is that of the Wild West, the cowboy, the Indian, and the sheriff. The historical actuality upon which it is based is sordid, meager, and short, extending only from the end of the Civil War to the spreading of the railroads into the cattle country—

thirty years at the most. And many of its actual heroes were murderous ruffians, ne'er-do-wells, and psychopaths.

But the actuality though fully documented has not prevented the myth from spreading over the entire world. It is more of a shaping force in the mores of today's young than most of the established religions. Why? Who can explain it? There have been many conjectures, but this much seems obvious: it presents a world of innocent moral certainty with its good guys and its bad guys. It lacks the complexity, perplexity, and confusion of our real lives in our industrial, urban civilization. Life in the westerns is all action; the noble hue of resolution is never there sicklied o'er with the pale cast of thought. In that glittering air, amid those sunburned mesas and sharp, upthrusting rocks everything is clearly marked, sharply delineated, there are no fogs or smogs ("never is heard a discouraging word/ And the skies are not cloudy all day"). The hero is self-reliant and self-assured. He pays no taxes or insurance premiums, receives no bills or traffic tickets, fears no unemployment (having, indeed, no visible employment), and is not subject to the draft. The gun resolves all difficulties and he is quick on the draw. He is rarely married and knows no domestic irritations or burdens. He has a sidekick, but the sidekick, though always there in emergencies, is comfortably admiring and inferior. And he can always be replaced by the horse. No wonder that hundreds of harassed millions the world over tune in on this dream, imitate its dress and walk.

On a higher literary level something of the same spaciousness and freedom draw us to the *Odyssey*. There is a morning freshness to it. It is a world of wind and wave and oar. There is the pungency of woodsmoke, the softness of thick fleeces. It is primitive but not barbaric. The power of the great leader is absolute but tempered by humanity and restrained by justice.

To those who first heard some bard sing the story of Odysseus' wanderings, it may very well have seemed pure history, an account of the adventures that befell the heroic king of Ithaca as he strove for ten years to regain his native land. The more sophisticated even then may have doubted the actuality of some of the monsters he encountered but they probably did not doubt that the narrative was true on the whole. And they assuredly did not doubt that the favor or disfavor of the gods could assist or impede a journey, could turn any human enterprise from success to disaster. Indeed our own fathers and grandfathers believed that, well into the twentieth century.

But the most thorough skeptic can still read the epic with delight and find in its fantasies profound relevances. The *Iliad*, as Simone Weil had so movingly written, is the poem of force, man reduced to matter by the impact of violence. It lies heavy on the heart. But the *Odyssey* is the saga of the mind, the epic of man seeking fulfillment. It fills the heart with exultation.

Odysseus' crowning greatness is his steadfastness, his unswerving adherence to his purpose. It does not matter that Ithaca is a barren rock. It holds his wife, his son, his father, his property, his duties. In brief, his life. And thither he will return. He cannot be debarred or deflected, intimidated or seduced. He is impervious to the pride of asceticism and to the demoralization of debauchery. His resolution carried him as safely past Circe as past Scylla. Calypso offered him immortality "but his heart yearned for the sight of his own hearthstone, and he wept by the gray sea shore."

Consider his brief sojourn with the Phaeacians. Dear to

them was the banquet and the harp and the dance and changes of raiment and the warm bath and love and sleep. They welcome him with honor and offer him the daughter of their king in marriage if he will consent to stay with them. This is a temptation that confronts almost every hero—especially today—as he nears the great goal. He will be "taken up" by the "best people." Compliments, honors, wealth—everything is his for the taking. But to take he must stop. In the estimate of the world he will be crowning his career with success. But he—and he alone—knows that Ithaca lies a day's journey further on and that in stopping at Phaeacia he will be as complete a failure as if he had given up the first day.

Or consider the Sirens. What they offered, it will be remembered, was knowledge. And the rocks on which they lay were white with the bones of men who had listened to their song, men who in the pursuit of some heroic idea had become lost in the labyrinth of theory and planning, had sunk the ends in the means and died in the dust of libraries. The hero wants knowledge that he can use. He will descend into hell to get it but will not be lured aside by vain speculations. He is not dull or stupid. He is curious and willing to listen; but he is lashed to the mast of his fixed intent.

The physical dangers that Odysseus faced—the Laestrygones, Polyphemus, Scylla, and so on—are wonderfully dramatic. But they do not appeal to the modern imagination as much as the more subtle dangers of Circe, Calypso, and the Oxen of the Sun. Not the least of these was the mild-eyed, melancholy Lotos-Eaters, offering the honey-sweet opiate of passivity, of renouncing struggle and conflict— "There is no joy but calm!"—how alluring and how fatal it has been to hundreds of millions! But Odysseus—the incarnation of Western Man—is not tempted or deceived. He binds the weaker man weeping beneath the benches and the others "sitting well in order, smote the gray sea water with their oars."

There is hardly any difficulty in the path of man, particularly of intellectual man, that is not presented in some incident in this great narrative. For a hundred generations it has held us fascinated.

There are those, of course, especially among the scholarly, to whom such interpretations of myths seem no more than a game. But it is a game that mankind has played for millennia and one of great importance. The Bible as read, for example, is in many places far removed from the Bible as written. But that does not lessen its poetic—which is often to say its religious—value to the reader, its stimulation to creative wonder. The burning bush, the pillars of cloud and fire, the still small voice, the rain upon the waste places of the earth, the "man" who wrestled with Jacob at the ford Jabbok—all of these serve but to make darkness visible. But they *do* make it visible.

So with the graceful Greek and robust Norse mythologies. They relate in poetry things that could never be conveyed in prose. They tell us how imaginative men once saw the unseeable and spoke of the unspeakable. And they are still among civilization's greatest possessions. Chemistry tells us, for instance, that the ocean is but water in which salt and other solids are dissolved. Astronomy and physics tell us that it yields to the gravitational pull of the moon. And psychology tells us that its beauty and mystery are projections of ourselves.

But we are men and these projections are all that really matters to us. Reality may be the Gorgon which, once glimpsed, would turn us to stone; we can view her only in the reflection of our shield, our human limitations. And it *does* make us less forlorn to

> Have sight of Proteus rising from the sea;
> Or hear old Triton blow his wreathed horn.

We will not find scientific or historical truth in mythology. But we will find poetic truth. And poetic truth may be all the truth that men will ever know.

CONTENTS

A NOTE ON CROSS-REFERENCES

Names that occur in entries for which there is also a main entry appear in CAPITALS and SMALL CAPITALS. This convention denotes that additional information can be obtained relevant to the entry in which the cross-reference appears. Such cross-references may or may not be preceded by *see*. The first word set in CAPITALS and SMALL CAPITALS indicates the name under which the cross-reference is alphabetized.

Dictionary of Mythology

Absyrtus

Son of Aeëtes and brother of Medea. To facilitate Jason's escape from Colchis, after he had obtained the Golden Fleece, Medea cut Absyrtus into pieces and strewed them in the way of her pursuing father.

See JASON, MEDEA.

Acastus

Son of Pelias and father of Laodamia. He was one of the Argonauts and took part in the Calydonian Boar Hunt. His wife falsely accused Peleus, king of the Myrmidons, of attempting to seduce her, and Acastus, in revenge, stole Peleus' magic sword. Peleus later defeated Acastus and killed Acastus and his wife.

Achaeans

One of the four branches of the Hellenic people, the others being the Aeolians, Dorians, and Ionians. They derived their names from the four sons of Hellen, the son of Deucalion, from whom the Greeks took the general names of Hellenes.

Achaeans is the Homeric name for the Greeks.

ACHATES

Achates

The faithful companion of Aeneas, so faithful that his name has become a term or trope (especially in the Vergilian phrase *fidus Achates* = "faithful Achates"), for a devoted friend and follower.

Achelous

A river god, tutelary deity of the largest river in Greece. He and Hercules fought over the love of DEIANIRA. In the course of the fight Achelous changed into a serpent and then into a bull. Hercules broke off one of his horns—which the goddess of plenty adopted as her symbol, the cornucopia.

In one myth Achelous was regarded as the father of the SIRENS, who were sometimes called the *Acheloides*.

Acheron

The river of woe, one of the five rivers surrounding the underworld in Greek mythology. The souls of the dead had to cross it. It was sometimes used as a term for the underworld in general.

Without proper burial the dead souls were not allowed to cross Acheron—hence the importance to the Greeks of proper burial rites. The ferryman was named CHARON. In some legends the souls crossed Acheron, in others they crossed the river Styx.

Achilles

One of the greatest of the Greek heroes who took part in the siege of Troy. He was the son of Peleus and the Nereid THETIS. He is a warrior of irresistible prowess but is subject to violent fits of anger, in which fits he is barbarically cruel. Indeed Homer announces, in the very first line of the *Iliad*, that the subject of his great epic is "the wrath of Peleus' son."

The most famous instance of this is his quarrel with Agamemnon over the maiden Briseis. When she is taken from him he sulks in his tent and refuses to fight until the death of his dearest friend, Patroclus, brings him to the battlefield seeking revenge. There he slays Hector and drags his body behind his chariot three times around the walls of Troy. Later, however, he is moved to generous pity when Priam, Hector's aged father, comes to beg his son's body so that it might receive due funeral rites.

One of the best-known stories about Achilles is that his mother, to make him invulnerable in battle, dipped him in the river Styx when he was a baby. During the process she held him by the heel and this remained his one vulnerable spot. He was killed by Paris (or Apollo disguised as Paris), who shot him in the heel with a poisoned arrow.

Acrisius

Father of DANAË. He was killed accidentally by a blow from a quoit thrown by his grandson PERSEUS, a happening which had been foretold by an oracle.

Actaeon

A great hunter who had the misfortune to come, while hunting, upon Artemis, the goddess of chastity, as she was bathing. She changed him into a stag and he was pursued and torn to pieces by his own dogs.

Admetus

King of Pherae. He was sick and an oracle stated that he would die unless someone offered to accept death in his place. His wife ALCESTIS offered herself and was being carried off to the underground when Hercules, a friend of Admetus, intervened and by force compelled death to let her remain alive.

[Milton's sonnet on his second wife—whom he married after he had become blind and who died within a year or so of the marriage—the sonnet beginning

> Methought I saw my late espoused saint
> Brought to me like Alcestis from the grave—

is based on this myth. As often, however, he uses a pagan myth to illuminate a Christian doctrine, a practice of which Doctor Johnson sternly disapproved.]

Adonis

A beautiful young man beloved by Aphrodite, he was killed by a wild boar. Aphrodite begged Zeus to restore him to life, but Persephone had also become enamoured of him and would not let him go until Zeus decreed that he should spend half of each year in the upper world and the other half in the underworld. In the spring the festival of his rebirth was celebrated, especially by women. He was also worshipped in Babylonia, under the name of *Tammuz,* and thence the cult spread into Palestine (Ezekiel 8) among "the dark idolatries of alienated Judah" (Milton).

Adrastus

The only one of the SEVEN AGAINST THEBES who survived the expedition. Ten years later he led the sons of the original Seven in a second attack against the city and this time captured it. However, his son was lost and Adrastus died of grief.

Aeacus

Son of Zeus and Aegina and the father of Peleus, hence the grandfather of Achilles. He was a man of so great piety that the gods allowed him to judge disputes between them and after his death appointed him one of the judges of the underworld.

See also MYRMIDONS.

Aeaea

The island of the sorceress CIRCE. Odysseus lived there with her for a year and she bore him a son, TELEGONUS.

Aëdon

Daughter of Pandareos. She envied her sister-in-law Niobe her six sons and six daughters (in some accounts seven sons and seven daughters, and in still others ten sons and ten daughters) and out of envious hatred resolved to kill one of them. But by mistake she killed Itylus (or Itys), her own and only child. In her grief she begged Zeus to let her cease to be a human being, and he changed her into a nightingale, in which form she forever voices her sorrow in plaintive melody.

Aeëtes

King of Colchis, where the Golden Fleece hung on a tree, guarded by a dragon. He was father of MEDEA and ABSYRTUS.

See also JASON, PHRIXUS AND HELLE.

AEGAEON

Aegaeon

Another name for BRIAREUS.

Aegeus

King of Athens and husband of Medea, by whom he had a son, Medus, the legendary ancestor of the Medes.

By an earlier union he was father of THESEUS and he killed himself when, owing to a mistake, he believed Theseus had been killed by the MINOTAUR. Theseus had gone to Crete with the tribute of young men and maidens which Athens was compelled to pay yearly to Minos. The ship, to suit its melancholy errand, was equipped with black sails. Theseus hoped to overcome the Minotaur—to which the young people were offered as victims—and had agreed to change to white sails if his expedition had a favorable outcome. But he forgot and Aegeus, seeing the black sails of the approaching vessel, threw himself into the sea (hence called the *Aegean*).

Some versions of the legend state that Theseus deliberately left the black sails hoisted (knowing the consequences) so that he could inherit the kingdom.

Aegis

The aegis was the shield of Zeus, made by Hephaestus and covered with the skin of the goat, AMALTHEA, which had suckled the infant Zeus. It was sometimes borne by Athena and when in her possession usually carried (veiled) the head of the Gorgon MEDUSA. When Zeus, the Thunderer, shakes the aegis, a thunderstorm ensues and men's hearts are seized with terror. It was sometimes represented as a shield and sometimes as a short, fringed cloak—the fringe presumably representing the trailing edges of the storm cloud. However represented, it was a manifestation of the awful power of

Zeus and Athena, a power used for protection as well as for warning.

[The most common meaning of the word today—aside from the specific mythological meaning—is that of a protective influence, usually of the favor of some powerful person.]

Aegisthus

Son of THYESTES and Pelopia (Thyestes' own daughter) and hence cousin of Agamemnon and Menelaus. While Agamemnon was absent at the siege of Troy, Aegisthus became the lover of CLYTEMNESTRA, Agamemnon's wife. In some accounts it is Aegisthus who killed Agamemnon on his return. In others it is Clytemnestra. After the murder they ruled the kingdom together until both were slain by ORESTES.

Aegyptus

Aegyptus had fifty sons and his twin brother DANAUS had fifty daughters, and the fifty sons demanded their fifty cousins in marriage. Danaus gave his daughters daggers with which forty-nine of them killed their husbands on the wedding night. In punishment for this, the Danaïdes were compelled to spend eternity trying to carry water in sieves. In one account the one daughter who did not kill her husband was Hypermnestra. Her husband was Lynceus and from their union sprang the royal house of Argos. In another it was Amymone.

[The idea of hell as eternal frustration is further illustrated by the fates of TANTALUS, IXION, and SISYPHUS. Robert Graves believes, however, that the idea of the Danaïdes' punishment is a late misunderstanding of an icon which, in reality, depicts them as sprinkling water in order to induce rain by sympathetic magic.]

AENEAS

Aeneas

Son of Anchises and the goddess Aphrodite, a famous Trojan leader. He is among the heroes in Homer's *Iliad* and is *the* hero of Vergil's *Aeneid*.

After the sack of Troy he fled the burning city, bearing his aged father on his back and leading his son Ascanius. Guided and protected by his divine mother, he finally (in the *Aeneid*) became the founder of Rome. Among the incidents that marked his wanderings, the most famous is his love affair with the Carthaginian queen, DIDO.

Aeolus

God of the winds. With his six sons and six daughters he lived, feasting eternally, on the bronze-bulwarked island of Aeolia, where he kept the winds chained. In the *Odyssey* he gave Odysseus a bull's hide within which all contrary winds were confined. But just as Odysseus and his crew came in sight of Ithaca, their homeland, Odysseus fell asleep and the men, thinking the leathern bag to contain a treasure, opened it and were swept by the released winds across the sea and none of them except Odysseus ever saw his homeland again.

[Until very recently it was widely believed among sailors that one could buy a favorable wind. Certain old women sold winds for sixpence in the Orkneys and the Hebrides as late as 1903. See *Folklore* XIV (1903), 302.]

Aesculapius (or Asclepius, Asklepios)

The god of medicine and healing. Son of Apollo and CORONIS. In the *Iliad* he is spoken of as a mortal who had learned his leechcraft from Chiron, the Centaur. He was killed by a thunderbolt because, in one version, he had violated the order of nature by restoring Hippolytus to life or, in another version,

8

because Hades had complained to Zeus that Aesculapius, by his skill, was preventing mankind from going, in the customary way, to the underworld.

He is represented as an old man with a beard, bearing a staff around which a serpent is entwined. This attribute, stylized, has become the emblem of the medical profession.

[The Greeks customarily offered a sacrifice to Aesculapius after recovering from an illness. Socrates' last words were addressed to his friend Crito to remind him that he "owed a cock to Aesculapius." Some see this as a recollection of a minor due piety, a little detail of life to be tidied up. Others read a deeper meaning and interpret it as a humorous way of saying that he has been cured of the disease of living, viewing death as the healing of all ills.]

Aesir

The collective name for the gods in Norse mythology.

Aeson

Father of JASON. He was denied his right to the throne of Thessaly by his half brother Pelias. MEDEA, returning from Colchis with Jason, contrived the death of Pelias and rejuvenated Aeson by boiling him in a magic concoction.

Aethra

The mother of Theseus.

Afterlife

Among the Greeks and Romans there was no clear, precise statement about an afterlife, though there are numerous contradictory assertions and beliefs. But most people seemed to have believed in some sort of continuation of identity and awareness after death.

AGAMEDES

The most general belief was that the dead (with a few, fortunate exceptions) existed together in a gloomy, subterranean abode ruled over by HADES and his consort PERSEPHONE. The existence experienced there was faint and cheerless.

See HADES, ELYSIUM.

Agamedes

See TROPHONIUS.

Agamemnon

Son of Atreus, grandson of Pelops, brother of Menelaus and hence brother-in-law of Helen. Doubly so, indeed, for he was the husband of her sister Clytemnestra, by whom he was the father of Orestes, Iphigenia, Electra, and Chrysothemis. He was the king of Argos, commander-in-chief of the Greek army against Troy.

He is represented as a brutal man, of great courage but irresolute, vindictive, cruel, and insolent. Intent on victory, he sacrificed his daughter IPHIGENIA in order to gain a favorable wind for his fleet. In the sack of Troy he permitted the shrines of the gods to be desecrated, and carried off, as a concubine, Cassandra, the priestess of Apollo. On his return to Argos he was murdered by Clytemnestra and her paramour AEGISTHUS.

Agave

Daughter of CADMUS and mother of PENTHEUS. Pentheus resisted the introduction of the worship of Dionysus, and Agave, in a Dionysian frenzy, tore him to pieces.

Agenor

1. Son of Poseidon and the father of CADMUS and EUROPA.
2. Half brother of Hector. He attempted to engage Achilles in

single combat and would have been killed had not Apollo intervened and rescued him.

Aglaia

One of the GRACES.

Aglauros

Sister of Herse who was beloved by Hermes. When Hermes visited Herse, Aglauros, who was jealous, got in his way and said she would not move. The god took her at her word and turned her into stone.

Agravain

A knight of King Arthur's Round Table. He was the son of King Lot and hence a nephew of King Arthur. He was the brother of Gawain, Gaheris, and Gareth. He hated Launcelot (who had accidentally killed Gaheris) and revealed Launcelot's illicit love for Guinevere to Arthur.

Ahriman

The leader of the powers of evil in Zoroastrian mythology. He is in constant conflict with Ahura Mazda, leader of the forces of good or of light.

Ajax (Greek **Aias**)

1. Ajax the son of Telamon ("the Telamonian Ajax"). A giant in size, he was the strongest of the Greek warriors in the Trojan War. But he was unintellectual and slow of speech. He fought Hector in single combat and, though he did not kill the greatest of the Trojans, had the better of the contest. When after the death of Achilles that hero's magnificent armor was awarded to Odysseus, Ajax went mad with anger and disappointment and killed himself. Later Odysseus encountered

ALASTOR

Ajax' shade in the underworld and tried to placate him, but the sullen ghost, still nursing his resentment, stalked away in speechless anger.

[Vergil in the *Aeneid* imitated Homer's depiction of the meeting of Odysseus and Ajax in the underworld by having Dido stalk away in indignant silence when Aeneas, also visiting the underworld, tried to soothe her shade. But, as Dr. Johnson observed, the imitation was unsuitable—because Ajax was not a man of words and hated Odysseus' glibness; whereas Dido was highly vocal.]

2. The Locrian Ajax (son of Oilus, king of the Locrians), sometimes called "the lesser Ajax." He was a brave fighter but a brutal and blasphemous man who at the sack of Troy desecrated the sacred Palladium and was finally drowned by Poseidon for uttering triumphant blasphemies as he scrambled ashore after a shipwreck.

Alastor

Son of Neleus and brother of Nestor. He married Harpalyce, daughter of Clymenus, who, moved by incestuous desire, kidnapped the bride from his son-in-law. She, to be revenged upon her father, killed her younger brother and served his cooked flesh to Clymenus. She prayed to be freed from the world of men and was changed into a bird. Alastor was later killed by Hercules.

Alberich

The tyrannical dwarf who in the *Nibelungenlied* guards the treasure of the Nibelungs. He owns the Tarnhelm, which confers invisibility, and the magic ring, which makes its possessor all-powerful. Loki and Wotan steal the ring, but Alberich has laid a curse upon it: "To no lord let it bring gain, and

let murder ever follow it until I hold it again in my hand."
And this curse falls upon whoever owns the ring.

See ANDVARI.

Alcestis

The daughter of Pelias and the wife of Admetus, king of
Pherae. He was seized with a mortal sickness and she offered to die in his place, Apollo having promised that Admetus need not die if anyone were willing to die for him. In
some versions of the story she was allowed to return to life
by Persephone, in others she was dragged back to earth by
Hercules.

[The legend is the subject of a play by Euripides and of a
moving comparison in Milton's sonnet *On His Deceased
Wife.*]

Alcides (= "son, or descendant, of Alcaeus")

A patronymic of Hercules, who was actually the son of Zeus.
Alcaeus was the father of his putative father AMPHITRYON.

[In former times when the idea of the family was much
stronger and more inclusive than it now is, kinship was often
expressed through the grandfather or some member of the
family in the larger sense. Thus until late into the seventeenth century *nephew,* though strictly a brother's or sister's
son, was often used for grandsons ("Grandmothers love
their nephews more than their own immediate children") or
for descendants of all kinds ("The Jews are Abraham's nephews").]

Alcinous

King of the PHAEACIANS, who, with his queen Arete and his
daughter Nausicaa and his son Laodamas, hospitably enter-

tains Odysseus and gives him rich gifts. He has Odysseus taken in the magic ship of the Phaeacians to Ithaca.

Alcippe

1. Daughter of Ares by Aglauros. She was raped by HALIR-RHOTHIUS, son of Poseidon, who was killed by Ares. A special court, the Areopagus (= "the hill of Ares"), was established to try Ares, who was condemned for the murder to undergo a period of serfdom.

[St. Paul "stood in the midst of Mars' hill" (Acts 17:22) and expounded the meaning of "the unknown god" to the Athenians. And John Milton made *Areopagitica* the title of his great essay defending freedom of speech (1644).]

2. Daughter of a son of Ares. She was the wife of Evenus and the mother of MARPESSA.

Alcmaeon

Son of Amphiaraus and Eriphyle. He led the EPIGONI in their successful expedition against Thebes. He avenged his father's death by murdering his mother, in punishment for which he was driven mad and pursued by the Furies. He married Arsinoë, daughter of Phegeus, but he abandoned her for Callirrhoë and Arsinoë's brothers killed him.

Alcmene

Wife of Amphitryon and mother, by Zeus, of HERCULES. By Amphitryon she had a son Iphicles, born, as a twin, with Hercules. At her death, which occurred after that of Hercules, she was taken to the Islands of the Blest. Odysseus saw her when he visited the underworld to consult the seer Tiresias.

Alfheim

The home of the elves or dwarfs in Norse mythology.

Aloeus

Father, by Iphimedia, of the giants OTUS AND EPHIALTES.

Alpheus

See ARETHUSA.

Amalthea

The nurse of Zeus. She is sometimes represented as a nymph, more often as a she-goat. After her death she was placed in the heavens as the constellation Capricorn.

Amata

Wife of King Latinus, in the *Aeneid*. She committed suicide when her daughter, Lavinia, who had been betrothed to Turnus, married Aeneas.

Amazons

A mythical nation or society of female warriors whose residence was thought to be various places on the outer borders of the world the Greeks knew. They provided for their continuance by meeting once a year with men of some other nation. The males born of this union were killed and the females at puberty had the right breast excised so that it would not impede the bowstring in battle. [This belief was due to an attempt to derive the word *amazon* from *a-(=* negative) + *mazos,* "breast." But it is pure folk-etymology.]

The Amazons played a large part in Greek mythology. In the *Iliad* they fought against Bellerophon and against Priam —though in other legends they came to Priam's aid after the death of Hector. Their queen, Penthesilea, was the daughter of Ares. She was slain by Achilles, who mourned for her and killed the boorish Thersites for ridiculing his grief. One of the feats of Hercules was obtaining the girdle of HIPPOLYTE, one of their queens.

[The Amazon River in South America was so called because it was rumored that a tribe of warrior women lived somewhere within its basin.]

See also HIPPOLYTE, HIPPOLYTUS.

Ambrosia and Nectar

Ambrosia was the food and nectar was the drink of the gods.

Ammon

Originally an Egyptian god, the god of the city of Thebes. He had a famous oracle at the temple of Siwa, which came, in time, to rival the greatest of the Greek oracles. Ammon came to be absorbed into Greek mythology. Called variously *Amen, Amon, Amun,* and (later, when incorporated with the sun god Ra) *Amon-Ra,* he was represented as a human body with a ram's head and large, curving horns. In Greek representations he was sometimes depicted with the head of Zeus with ram's horns.

[Ammonia (which was a woman's name as recently as mideighteenth century) derives its name from the fact that sal ammoniac was obtained from camel dung near the great shrine of Amon in Libya.]

Amphiaraus

A hero of Argos who took part in the Argonautic expedition, the hunt for the Calydonian Boar, and the campaign of the Seven Against Thebes. He was a seer and, foreknowing the ill-fated result of the expedition against Thebes, would have nothing to do with it until compelled to by his wife Eriphyle, sister of ADRASTUS. She had been bribed with the necklace of HARMONIA.

He set out but commanded his children to avenge his death on Eriphyle and, later, to make another attack on Thebes. Worsted in an action before the Homoloian gate at Thebes, he fled and was swallowed up in a chasm in the ground opened by a thunderbolt from Zeus. This was, apparently, a way of saving him so that he might be translated to Elysium. A shrine and oracle was erected on the spot of his engulfment.

Amphion

Son of Zeus and ANTIOPE and twin brother of Zethus. The brothers captured Thebes and killed King Lycus and his queen, Dirce, who had ill-treated their mother. They rebuilt the walls of Thebes. Zethus, possessed of great strength, rolled huge stones into place. Amphion, playing on the lyre given to him by the god Hermes, caused even greater stones to roll into place of their own accord. Amphion married NIOBE and after Apollo killed all of their children he committed suicide.

Amphitrite

A Nereid, the wife of Poseidon and mother of Triton. She had a golden palace in the depths of the sea.

Amphitryon

Son of Alcaeus and husband of Alcmene. She bore twins: Iphicles to Amphitryon and Hercules to Zeus (who had seduced her by assuming the semblance of Amphitryon, who was, at the time, away on a journey).

Other episodes in Amphitryon's life concern his catching the Teumession vixen and his affair with Comaetho. In the first of these, to gain the military aid of Creon, king of Thebes, he agreed to catch the uncatchable fox, using the infallible hound which Minos had given to Procris, wife of Cephalus of Athens. Zeus solved the insoluble problem by turning both fox and hound into stone. In the second, he warred with Pterelaus, king of the Teleboans and grandson of Poseidon. Pterelaus had a lock of golden hair which assured him of immortality but his daughter Comaetho fell in love with Amphitryon and, seeking to please him, plucked out her father's golden lock. But Amphitryon had her put to death for parricide.

[The term *amphitryon* is used throughout literature to designate a host, or the true host, the one who is actually paying for the feast. This is derived from an incident in this story in which Zeus—the seeming Amphitryon—is giving a banquet when the true Amphitryon unexpectedly returns. The idea of a god cuckolding a mortal by assuming his form appealed to the comic dramatists and this legend has been dramatized by Plautus, Molière, Dryden, Giraudoux, and (it is estimated) some thirty-four other playwrights.]

Amycus

Son of Poseidon by the Hamadryad Melia, Amycus was king of the Bebrycians. A brutal man of enormous strength, he insisted that all strangers box with him. He had the misfortune, however, on the arrival of the Argonauts, to be matched with Polydeuces, who after a bloody bout managed to kill him.

Amymone

One of the Danaïdes, the only one who murdered her husband and nevertheless escaped eternal punishment. And this was chiefly because she was loved by Poseidon, who caused a spring to flow in Argos, where he had, in answer to her cries for help, saved her from a satyr. By Poseidon she had a son, NAUPLIUS.

Anaxarete

A cruel virgin who caused her lover, IPHIS, to kill himself. The gods turned her into a stone.

Ancaeus

An Arcadian, son of Poseidon and pilot of the *Argo*. There are two accounts of his death:

(1) that he received a mortal wound from the Calydonian Boar;

(2) that he was killed driving a wild boar—just an ordinary wild boar—out of his vineyard. In this version, just as he had raised a cup of wine to his lips a servant foretold that he would never live to taste it. And at the same second news was brought of the boar's intrusion. Ancaeus threw away the cup and rushed to oppose the boar and met his death in the attempt.

Anchises

Father of Aeneas by Aphrodite. It was Aeneas' care for his aged father, whom he bore on his shoulders as he fled from burning Troy, that earned Aeneas the sobriquet of "the pious Aeneas," piety having in Latin the particular meaning of "du-

tiful in relation to one's parents." Anchises did not reach
Italy with his heroic son but died in Sicily.

[Cf. Wordsworth's:

> The Child is father of the Man;
> And I could wish my days to be
> Bound each to each by natural piety.]

Ancile

See NUMA POMPILUS.

Androgeus

Son of Minos, king of Crete, and his queen Pasiphaë. Androgeus visited Athens and won every contest in the Athenian
games. This aroused the jealousy of King AEGEUS, who had
the young man murdered. Some accounts say it was simply
by ambush. Others say, Aegeus sent him to fight the
Marathonian Bull, the equivalent of a death sentence. Minos
avenged Androgeus' death by compelling the Athenians to
send seven youths and seven maidens to Crete every nine
years to be devoured by the Minotaur.

Andromache

Wife of Hector, who—like her father and brothers—was
killed by Achilles. After Troy had been taken, her son Astyanax was put to death by the victorious Greeks and she was
given as a slave to Neoptolemus (by whose wife, Hermione,
she was almost killed).

Andromeda

Daughter of Cepheus and Cassiopeia. Cassiopeia had boasted
that she was more beautiful than the Nereids, and Poseidon,
offended, had sent a sea monster to ravage the country. The

monster could be diverted from utter destruction of the land only by Andromeda's being offered to him and, accordingly, she was chained to a rock on the seashore. She was rescued, however, by Perseus, who passed by on his return from decapitating Medusa. He killed the monster and turned her uncle and others, who opposed his marrying the maiden, into stone by exposing the head of the Medusa. Perseus, Andromeda, Cassiopeia, and even the monster were dignified by being turned into constellations (the monster = Cetus).

Andvaranaut

The accursed ring made by the dwarf king Andvari. It was given to Brunhild by Sigurd when they were betrothed and taken from her when he was wooing her for Gunnar. Gudrun sent it to her brothers to warn them (in vain) against coming to Atli's court.

Andvari

The guardian of treasures in the *Volsung Saga*. In the *Nibelungenlied* he is called ALBERICH.

Angerona

The Roman goddess of secret sorrow whose rites were celebrated on December 21 in the temple of Volupia, the goddess of pleasure. Little is known of her aside from a mention in Macrobius.

[Macrobius was quoted in Burton's *Anatomy of Melancholy,* whence Keats drew one of his most famous passages:

> Aye, in the very temple of Delight
> Veil'd Melancholy has her sovran shrine.

Actually the goddess was not veiled, but was represented with her mouth bound and sealed.]

Animals

Various animals were sacred to or closely connected with various mythological figures. Thus the cow with Hera, the bull with Dionysus, the horse with Poseidon. In Roman mythology the wolf was associated with Mars.

See also BIRDS.

Antaeus

The giant son of Poseidon and Earth who forced all who passed to wrestle with him and invariably killed them, until Hercules killed him by holding him aloft, out of contact with the strength-giving Earth, until his strength ebbed.

Antenor

One of the elders of Troy. He disapproved of Paris' abduction of Helen and urged that she be given back to Menelaus. The Greeks spared him when Troy was sacked and, possibly because of this, he was, in some accounts, regarded as a traitor. He was accused by some of having helped the Greeks to steal the Palladium and even to have opened the door of the Wooden Horse.

Anteros

The son of Aphrodite and hence the brother of EROS, Anteros represented mutual love and was sometimes regarded as the avenger of slighted love. There was also a third brother—Himeros—who represented the longings of love.

Anticlea

The daughter of Autolycus, wife of Laertes and mother of Odysseus. Odysseus sees her shade when he descends to Hades to question Tiresias. She tells him that she had died of grief at his long absence.

Antigone

The daughter (and sister) of Oedipus who accompanied him in his wanderings after he had been driven out of Thebes in expiation of his unwitting patricide and incest. After Oedipus' death she returns to Thebes, where in defiance of the order of King Creon she gives her dead brother Polynices the rites of burial. In consequence of this, even though she is betrothed to Haemon, Creon's son, she is immured in a cave, or vault, where she takes her own life.

Antilochus

The son of Nestor, a brave warrior and a skilled charioteer. It is he, in the *Iliad,* who brings Achilles the news of the death of Patroclus.

Antinous

He appears in the *Odyssey.* He is the chief and most insolent of the suitors for Penelope's hand.

Antiope

Daughter of the river god Asopus and mother by Zeus of the twin Theban heroes Amphion and Zethus. They were taken from her while still infants and reared by a herdsman. Fleeing from the persecution of Dirce, wife of King Lycus, Antiope found but did not recognize her sons. Dirce overtook her and ordered her to be bound to the horns of a wild bull and dragged to death. The herdsman, however, revealed her identity, and her sons bound Dirce to the bull's horns and had *her* dragged to death.

Antiphates

The king of the giant Laestrygones who, in the *Odyssey*, eats one of Odysseus' heralds and whose people destroy all of Odysseus' fleet and men except the one vessel and its crew in which the hero himself manages to escape.

Anubis

The jackal-headed god of the dead in Egyptian mythology. He was particularly the god of embalming and the guardian of tombs. In Greek mythology he came to be identified with Hermes and was called *Hermanubis*.

Aphrodite

The Greek goddess of love, not merely of sex but of affection and all the impulses that bind men together in social communion. In some accounts she was the daughter of Zeus and a Titan. In the best-known and most poetic account, she arose from the sea-foam. Her equivalent in Roman mythology, Venus, is more directly sexual. Many scholars view her as a manifestation of the Phoenician goddess Astarte.

She sometimes appears as the wife of Hephaestus (Vulcan), the mother of Eros (Cupid), the lover of Ares (Mars), and the one to whom Paris awarded the golden apple inscribed "for the fairest." Her bribe or reward for this—the gaining for him of Helen's love—precipitated the Trojan War.

By Anchises, Aphrodite was the mother of Aeneas.

APPLES OF THE HESPERIDES

Apis

The sacred bull in Egyptian mythology. In it the god Osiris was believed to be incarnate.

Apollo

The son of Zeus and Leto and brother of Artemis, one of the greatest of the Olympian gods. He was the god of the intellect, of the arts, of healing, and of light. His greatest shrine was that of the famous oracle at Delphi, which he had gained by killing the Python, a dragon which had formerly guarded the place.

Of his loves, noteworthy is that for Coronis, the mother of Aesculapius; of Daphne, whom he turned into a laurel; of Cassandra, to whom he gave the gift of prophecy—which he could not recall but which, when she denied him her love, he nullified by decreeing that, although she should foretell the future, no one would ever believe her. A somewhat similar legend concerned the Cumaean Sibyl. She asked to live as many years as she could hold grains of sand in her hands and he granted her wish, but when she denied him her favors he refused to attach eternal youth to her eternal years and she grew incredibly shrivelled and longed for death.

Apples of the Hesperides

Titaea, an earth goddess, presented Zeus and Hera, at their marriage, with a tree that bore golden fruit. The divine pair were greatly pleased with this gift and placed it in the care of the HESPERIDES. But the nymphs ate some of the fruit and to prevent this the serpent Ladon was set to guard the tree. Hercules, as his eleventh labor, killed the serpent and carried off some of the golden apples. He didn't pluck the apples himself but persuaded Atlas to do it for him. Atlas was condemned to hold up the sky. Hercules relieved him of this crushing burden and Atlas was tricked, after he had obtained the apples, into reassuming it. Hercules took the apples to Eurystheus, who gave them back to him. Hercules then gave them to Athena, who showed her wisdom by returning them to the Hesperides, since they—the apples—were the property of Hera, a goddess jealous of her rights and not to be trifled with.

Arachne

A foolish woman who, proud of her great skill in weaving, presumptuously challenged the goddess Athena to a competition and was changed by the indignant goddess into a spider.

Arcadia

A pastoral, mountainous country in the central Peloponnesus, distinguished for its rustic simplicity and the innocence of its inhabitants. It early became and has long remained a trope for the idyllic.

Arcas

Son of Zeus and the Arcadian nymph Callisto. His grandfather, LYCAON, to test Zeus' omniscience, killed the boy and served up his flesh to Zeus—who destroyed the house with a thunderbolt, restored Arcas to life and changed Lycaon into a wolf.

Hera, who pursued many of the objects of Zeus' love with animosity, changed Callisto into a bear. Arcas, out hunting, would have killed her had not Zeus intervened and changed them into the constellations of the Great and Little Bear.

Archemorus

The infant son of the Nemean king Lycurgus. Originally named *Opheltes,* the child was placed in the care of Hypsipyle, who left it unattended one day while she showed the SEVEN (AGAINST THEBES) a spring of water. Returning, she found her charge dead, killed by a serpent. The seer Amphiaraus renamed the dead child Archemorus (= "the beginning of trouble") and identified the serpent as an evil omen sent by Zeus.

[The changing of the name obviously did the dead child no good, but it might have diverted an evil omen. That is, a sign dispatched to the Seven through Opheltes could not be delivered, as it were, because there wasn't any Opheltes; there was only an Archemorus and he was dead. The omen would have to be returned "addressee unknown."]

Ares (Roman **Mars**)

Son of Zeus and Hera, Ares, the god of war, is brutal, ferocious, and blustering. He delighted in slaughter and the sacking of cities, but was cowardly and fled to Zeus for protection when Diomedes wounded him. Except for his sister, Eris, the goddess of discord, and Aphrodite, all of the immortals hated him. With Aphrodite he had an illicit love affair which produced three children: Phobus, Deimus, and Harmonia. It also produced one of the greatest scandals on Olympus, for Hephaestus, husband of Aphrodite, warned by Helios of what was going on, made a subtle net which exposed the lovers in *flagrante delicto.* The gods crowded in to see them and there was great merriment at the spectacle—though the goddesses modestly stayed away. Zeus was disgusted. Hephaestus threatened to divorce her but loved her too much to do so.

ARETHUSA

Ares was implicated in another undignified affair when OTUS AND EPHIALTES, fun-loving juvenile giants, imprisoned him in a bronze jar for thirteen months.

Arethusa

A nymph attendant upon Artemis who, when pursued by the river god Alpheus, was changed by her mistress into a fountain on the island of Ortygia. Alpheus, in his determination, was thought to flow under the sea to the island to mingle his waters with hers.

[The god Alpheus may be alluded to, by a sort of echo in Coleridge's *Kubla Khan:*

> Where Alph, the sacred river, ran
> Through caverns measureless to man
> Down to a sunless sea.

The supposition finds some support from the fact that in his brief explanatory note to this poetic fragment Coleridge quotes from Theocritus, the Greek pastoral poet.]

Argo

The ship of the Argonauts, built by Argos the Thespian. Athena aided him with advice and fixed in the bows a piece of wood from the sacred oak at Dodona (*see* ORACLES), which had the power of speech.

Argonauts

The Argonauts were the heroes who in the ship *Argo* sailed, under the command of Jason, to Colchis to seize and bring back to King Pelias the Golden Fleece. The famous band— for the expedition was one of the greatest of the Greek sagas —included Hercules, Orpheus, Argos (who built the ship), and a score of other legendary figures. At Colchis they were set various tasks: yoking fire-breathing bulls, sowing the famous dragon's teeth, etc. Jason, aided by Medea, finally got the fleece and fled with it.

Argos

1. The kingdom of Agamemnon.
2. The man who built the *Argo,* the ship in which the Argonauts sailed for the Golden Fleece.

Argus

1. A many-eyed monster (accounts vary from three to one hundred eyes) who was set by Hera to watch Io after Zeus, to conceal his relations with her, had changed her into a heifer. Zeus had Hermes kill Argus, and Hera then turned him into a peacock.
2. The aged, faithful hound of Odysseus who alone immediately recognized his master when, after twenty years' absence, the hero returned in disguise to his own house. The loyal creature merely had time to thump his tail in recognition before he died, his life fulfilled. He was possibly so called because as a watchdog he rivalled Argus 1.

[Byron (*Don Juan* III, xxiii), commenting on the dangers of long voyages from home, says:

> An honest gentleman at his return
>   May not have the good fortune of Ulysses
> • • • • • • • • • • • • • • • •
> The odds are that he finds a handsome urn
>   To his memory—and two or three young misses
> Born to some friend, who holds his wife and riches;—
> And that *his* Argus bites him by—the breeches.]

ARIADNE

Ariadne

Daughter of Minos and Pasiphaë and sister of Phaedra. She fell in love with Theseus and supplied him with the clew of thread that permitted him to escape from the Labyrinth after he had killed the Minotaur. She fled with him as he returned to Athens, but he abandoned her on the island of Naxos ("leaving upon her sad knee/ This Adriatic Ariadne"—Byron). She found solace for her abandonment in the love of Dionysus (Bacchus).

[Keats, presumably on the authority of his own poetic imagination, insisted that Bacchus always kept a cellar of very fine claret for Ariadne's exclusive use.]

Arimaspians

A legendary northern people who lived next to the Hyperboreans. They had but one eye and their whole life was a continual warfare with griffins who protected a hoard of gold.

Arion

1. The horse which Hercules gave to Adrastus. It was begotten by Poseidon upon Demeter or, in other accounts, sprang into being when Poseidon struck the earth with his trident (though these, of course, are the same story in different symbols). Two of its feet were human feet. It had the power of speech and ran with miraculous speed.

2. A musician who flourished at the court of Periander in the sixth century B.C. He enters the realm of mythology because of the legend that on being thrown overboard, on a voyage from Sicily to Corinth, he was carried safely to land by a dolphin that was charmed by his playing of the lyre.

Aristaeus

Son of Apollo and Cyrene. He was protector of cattle and fruit trees and a developer of bee culture. It was in flight from his advances that EURYDICE trod upon a snake and was bitten in the foot and died.

Artemis (Roman **Diana**)

Daughter of Zeus and Leto, twin sister of Apollo. A virgin huntress goddess, she is usually represented in a tucked-up gown with a bow and a quiver of arrows. She was the goddess of chastity and had the power of inflicting or healing sickness. She was particularly connected with childbirth (having assisted her mother Leto with the delivery of Apollo a few moments after her own birth) and was the protectress of the unborn and the newly born. One of the reasons given for her creating an adverse wind to detain Agamemnon and the Grecian army at Aulis was that he had killed a hare that was big with young. As a goddess of birth she became connected with the lunar cycle and hence was a moon goddess.

One of the great Olympians, she became identified with Hecate and Selene and passed even into the Bible as Diana of the Ephesians (Acts 19). Under the name of *Agrotera* she was the patron of huntsmen. In Arcadia, under the name *Calliste,* she was worshipped as a bear.

Arthur

Son of UTHER PENDRAGON and IGRAINE. Conceived (as a result of a strategy by the wizard Merlin) out of wedlock. Arthur was reared by Merlin. By pulling the magic sword Excalibur (sometimes *Caliburn*) from a stone from which no one else could extract it, he revealed himself, though then but a child, as the fated ruler of the kingdom. He was crowned, at the age of fifteen, in Wales and immediately defeated a league of eleven hostile kings, led by King Lot, King Nantres, and King Uriens, all three husbands of Arthur's three sisters.

Against Merlin's advice Arthur married GUINEVERE, who loved LAUNCELOT and was untrue to Arthur. He established his court at Camelot, where his knights were seated at the famous ROUND TABLE. A rebellion against him was raised by Modred (or Mordred), son of MORGAN LE FAY, Arthur's sister. Though Modred was thus ostensibly Arthur's nephew, he was actually his illegitimate son—though at the time of Modred's conception Arthur had not known that Morgan le Fay was his sister. A great battle is fought. Modred is killed. The knights of the Round Table are destroyed and Arthur is mortally wounded. Excalibur is thrown into a mere and three queens in black come on a barge to bear Arthur to Avalon.

Ascalaphus

The witness who testified that he had seen Persephone eat the pomegranate seeds and thus prevented her from returning from the lower world. Persephone turned him into an owl.

Ascanius

The son of Aeneas who accompanied his father to Italy after the fall of Troy. The Romans also called him *Iulus*.

Asgärd

The dwelling or city of the gods in Norse mythology. It included Valhalla, the great hall in Gladsheim, the palace of Odin and the twelve principal gods.

Ask and Embla

In Norse mythology the first man and woman. He was created out of an ash and she out of an elm. Odin gave them breath, Ve gave them feeling, and Vili gave them reason.

Asmodeus

A Zoroastrian demon who in the apocryphal book of Tobit is driven into Egypt by a magic charm made by Tobias of the burned heart and liver of a fish.

Astarte

A Phoenician goddess of love and fecundity, the Semitic equivalent of the Greek Aphrodite. She was associated with the moon and often depicted standing in a crescent moon.

Astolat

Elaine, the Lily Maid of Astolat. She died for love of Sir Launcelot.

[The story, in Malory's *Morte d'Arthur*, is the basis (together with Plato's famous image of the cave!) of Tennyson's *The Lady of Shalott*.]

Astraea

See DICE.

Astyanax

The young son of Hector and Andromache who, after the capture of Troy, was killed by being flung from the walls by the Greeks.

ATALANTA

Atalanta

1. The Arcadian Atalanta. A famous huntress, in some versions the daughter of Zeus by Clymene, in others daughter of Iasius, of the race of Callisto. She was suckled by a bear and took part in the hunt for the CALYDONIAN BOAR.

2. The Boeotian Atalanta, daughter of Schoeneus of Boeotia. She refused to marry any man who could not outdistance her in a footrace. The terms were that the suitor should have a short start, and if she could overtake him—and she was fleet of foot—she would plunge a spear into his back. She was finally won by Hippomenes, who, as she overtook him, flung down severally three golden apples, which she paused to pick up and so lost the race.

[To non-heroes the lady seems highly unattractive—a murderous hoyden whose lust for homicide is exceeded only by her greed! Some accounts give Melanion, son of Amphidamas, as the luckless winner. Later both were changed to lions, either because they had violated a sanctuary or because the groom forgot to thank Aphrodite for the golden apples of delay.]

Ate

The goddess of rashness and infatuation, of sudden impulses that lead men to ruin. She was swift of foot and ran before men to lead them to disaster. It was upon her that Agamemnon lay the blame for his quarrel with Achilles, the quarrel that almost lost the Greeks the Trojan War.

Athamas

Brother of Sisyphus, descended from Aeolus. He married Nephele, by whom he had Phrixus and Helle, the children who were flown across the strait separating Asia from Europe on the back of the ram with the Golden Fleece. The girl, Helle, fell from the ram as they crossed the strait (thereafter called the *Hellespont)* and was drowned.

Athamas turned Nephele away and married Ino, daughter of Cadmus. He went mad and she, fleeing from him, sprang (with her child Melicertes in her arms) into the sea. The gods made her a sea nymph under the name of LEUCOTHEA and the child a sea divinity under the name of PALAEMON.

Athena (also **Athene;** Roman **Minerva**)

The virgin goddess of wisdom and the arts and the special protectress of Athens. She was not born in the usual sense, but sprang into being fully formed and fully armed and uttering her war cry, from the forehead of Zeus. She wore the aegis and carried an invincible spear. Sacred to her were the owl and the olive tree.

She was a warrior goddess but not the goddess of war. The Greeks apparently conceived of wisdom as militant but not quarrelsome. Athena was always on the side of the victor—or, rather, her side always won because wisdom did not encourage rash engagements against hopeless odds. Ares was simply the god of battle and, as such, personified victory and defeat, valor and cowardice. But Athena was invulnerable and endured or encouraged strife only as a means to peace.

It would be easy to see her birth as an allegory of wisdom springing from the forehead of god and as such, no doubt, it may be accepted. But the full myth (or myths) is much more involved. Various legends attribute her parentage to a winged giant and to Poseidon. But the commonest legend is that Zeus got the Titaness Metis with child. An oracle told him that this child would be female but that the next one she conceived would be a son who would overthrow him as he had overthrown his father Cronus, who had overthrown *his*

ATLANTIS

father Uranus. Zeus, alarmed, put an end to this possibility by swallowing Metis, pregnant as she was. Soon after he developed a severe headache. Hermes persuaded Hephaestus (or, in some accounts, Prometheus) to split Zeus' skull with an axe and out sprang Athena, shouting.

[Athena is more than mere wisdom or cleverness. Metis, her mother, was cleverness—now forever embellied in Zeus; Athena is wisdom springing from power and deep experience, produced in love and fear and pain. The idea lends itself to endless poetic expansion.]

Atlantis

A mythical island believed to have sunk beneath the waves in some cataclysm of nature. It has been variously located off the Strait of Gibraltar, in the region of the Azores and, by some, it has been associated with Santorin, in the Cyclades.

It is referred to in Plato's *Timaeus* and *Critias*.

Atlas

A Titan, the son of Iapetus and Clymene. As punishment for his part in the war against the gods, he stands in the far west and supports the sky upon his mighty shoulders. He is the father of the Pleiads and, in some accounts, of the Hesperides and of Calypso.

When Hercules was seeking the Golden Apples of the HESPERIDES, he took the burden of the sky upon his own shoulders while the Titan fetched the apples for him. Atlas brought back the apples but had so enjoyed his freedom that he refused to resume his burden. But Hercules tricked him into it by asking him to hold the sky again only until Hercules could fix a cushion for his own head to ease the weight. Atlas agreed but, of course, found himself unable to lay that burden down when Hercules didn't keep *his* word but went on his way with the apples.

[It is characteristic of giants in folklore to be stupid and gullible—as was the giant in *Jack the Giant Killer.* Perhaps it reflects the boy's contempt—still mingled with fear—of his father.]

Atli

King of the Huns in the *Volsung Saga.* He demanded Gudrun, Sigurd's widow, for his wife. He treacherously murdered her brothers and was, in turn, murdered by her.

Atreus

Grandson of Tantalus, son of Pelops, brother of Thyestes, and the father of Agamemnon and Menelaus. He was the king of Mycenae.

Thyestes seduced his brother's wife, and Atreus, to be revenged, killed two of Thyestes' sons and served them as food to their father, an act so dreadful that the sun turned backwards in its course that day and would not pass over the ill-fated house in which such a deed was taking place. Thyestes' sole surviving son, Aegisthus (conceived in the incestuous union of Thyestes with his daughter Pelopia), seduced Clytemnestra, Agamemnon's wife, and helped her to kill Agamemnon on his return from Troy. In turn he was killed by Orestes, Agamemnon's son.

Attis

Son of the Lydian supreme god, Manes, and beloved by the Phrygian goddess Cybele.

In one version of his legend he was, like Adonis, killed by a boar and in the spring, in an orgiastic ritual, his followers sought him in the mountains. On the third day he was found and the finding celebrated with wild rejoicing. A more common version is that he fell in love and wished to marry, but Cybele, jealous, drove him mad and he castrated himself beneath a pine tree. The tree received his spirit and violets grew from his blood.

Audhumbla

The gigantic cow, born of the mist, whose milk nourished the primal Frost Giant Ymir. Audhumbla nourished herself by licking blocks of ice and from this licking was produced Bori, the original of all the Norse gods.

Augean Stables

As his fifth labor, Hercules undertook to cleanse the stables of Augeas, king of Elis. Augeas had three thousand oxen and the stables had not been cleaned in thirty years. Shovelling was out of the question, since the daily accretion far exceeded any possibility of such removal. Hercules solved the task by diverting two rivers so that they flowed through the stables. Augeas had promised Hercules a tenth of the herd if he performed the task—as he boasted he would—in one day. But when Hercules completed the task within the agreed time, Augeas refused to pay, on the ground that the cleansing was actually the work of the river gods. In some accounts Hercules let this sophistry (or rightful attribution!) pass; in others he returned later, waged war, and killed Augeas and his sons.

Aulis

The place of assembly of the Achaean fleet just before the expedition sailed for Troy. It was here that Agamemnon sacrificed his daughter Iphigenia in order to gain a favorable wind. This pacified the goddess Artemis (whom Agamemnon had offended) but it added fuel to the hatred felt for him by his wife Clytemnestra. Some versions say that Artemis snatched Iphigenia away at the last second and left a hind in her place.

[Tennyson in the first version (1832) of *A Dream of Fair Women* had Iphigenia describe her own death:

> One drew a sharp knife through my tender throat
> Slowly,—and nothing more

Lockhart, reviewing the poem for the *Quarterly Review,* said: "What touching simplicity! . . . *He cut my throat—Nothing more!* One might indeed ask *what more she would have."* Tennyson, nettled, changed the lines in the next edition (1842) to read:

> The bright death quiver'd at the victim's throat—
> Touch'd—and I knew no more.]

Aurora

See Eos.

Autolycus

The son of Hermes and the maternal grandfather of Odysseus. He "swore false and stole better than anyone else in the world." He had the power of making himself and his stolen goods invisible or of changing the appearance of the goods so they could not be identified.

Avalon

An earthly paradise in the western seas, ruled over by Morgan le Fay, to which King Arthur was taken after having received his death wound. Malory calls it "the isle of Avalon" and Tennyson calls it the "island-valley of Avilion."

Avernus

Now a small lake in the crater of an extinct volcano west of Naples, it was formerly believed to be the entrance to Hades. The CUMAEAN SIBYL had her grotto there and there were the grove of Hecate and the home of the Cimmerians. It is said that mephitic vapors exhaled from the lake killed birds flying over it and it owed its reputation to that fact.

[It is best known today from the famous lines in the sixth book of the *Aeneid*:

> *Facilis descensus Averni:*
> *Noctes atque dies patet atri ianua Ditis;*
> *Sed revocare gradum superasque evadere ad auras,*
> *Hoc opus, hic labor est.*

(Easy is the descent to Avernus:/ Night and day the portals of Dis stand open;/ But to recall thy step and return to the upper air/ —that is work, that is labor.)]

Azrael

The Islamic angel of death.

Bacchae

See MAENADS.

Bacchus

See DIONYSUS.

Bagdemagus

One of the knights of the Arthurian legends. He is offended because Sir Tor is raised to the dignity of the Round Table. He finds a sign of the Grail and finds Merlin sealed in a cave by the maid NINEVE but is unable to free him.

Balder

The most beautiful of the Norse gods, perhaps a personification of the sun. He was the son of Odin and Frigga, the husband of Nanna, and the father of Forseti. Balder dreamt that he would die and Frigga exacted from all things a promise that they would not harm him. But she overlooked the mistletoe and Loki, the eternal troublemaker, persuaded the blind god HODER to throw a sprig of mistletoe at Balder— who dropped dead when it struck him. The Aesir sent to Hel beseeching her to let Balder return from the dead, and this she agreed to do if all things, living and inanimate, wept for Balder. But an old hag, the giantess Thaukt (who some say

BALIN AND BALAN

was Loki in disguise) refused to weep and Balder could not return.

Balin and Balan

Brothers and knights of the Round Table who in Malory's *Morte d'Arthur* meet death at each other's hand unwittingly.

[Tennyson made them the subject of one of the *Idylls of the King* and Swinburne wrote "A Tale of Balen."]

Balmung

Siegfried's sword—with which Kriemhild cut off Hagen's head.

Ban

King of Brittany in Malory's *Morte d'Arthur*. He was the father of Sir LAUNCELOT.

Banshee

The English pronunciation and spelling of a Celtic phrase meaning "a woman of the elves or fairies." Such a spirit, attached to a certain family, could be heard wailing at the death of a member of the family.

Baucis

See PHILEMON.

Bedivere

A knight of the Round Table in Malory's *Morte d'Arthur*. He and his brother Lucan alone survived the great last battle. Sir Bedivere, at Arthur's command, threw EXCALIBUR into the water and bore Arthur to the barge where three veiled, wailing women waited to bear him to the Vale of Avalon.

Bellerophon

Son of Glaucus, king of Corinth, and grandson of Sisyphus. He rode Pegasus, the winged horse, slew the monster Chimera, and defeated the Amazons. He angered the gods—perhaps through pride. One legend has it that he attempted to mount to heaven on Pegasus. At any rate, Zeus had a gadfly sting the horse and Bellerophon was unseated and fell to his death.

Bellona

The Roman goddess of war, sometimes conceived of as the sister, and at other times the wife, of Mars.

Beowulf

King of the Geats in the eighth-century Anglo-Saxon poem that bears his name. About two-thirds of the poem's three thousand lines deals with the hero's fierce battles with—and slayings of—the troll-monster Grendel and Grendel's mother, freeing the Danish royal hall from their depredations. Later the hero defends his own people against a dragon. He kills the dragon but is himself slain in the struggle.

Bercilak de Hautdesert

The Green Knight.
  See GAWAIN.

Bestla

The wife of Bor and the mother of Odin and of his brothers Vili and Ve.

BIFROST

Bifrost

The Rainbow Bridge which, in Norse mythology, spanned the air from the earth to Asgärd, the home of the gods. Despite the fact that the red in the bridge's spectrum is fire, it is guarded day and night against an onrush of the Frost Giants by the sleepless Heimdal. Nonetheless at Ragnarok (the final destruction of the gods) the bridge is broken down.

Birds

Various birds were sacred to or commonly associated with various mythological figures. Thus the eagle was the bird of Zeus, the peacock of Hera, the owl of Athena, the swan of Apollo, the cock of Hermes. And sparrows and doves were the birds of Aphrodite.

Bona Dea

The Roman goddess of chastity and fecundity. She was the female equivalent of Faunus and was also known under the name *Fauna, Maia,* or *Ops.* She was worshipped solely by women. A scandal that affected the course of Roman history was caused by the appearance (in December, 62 B.C.) of the gangster-politician Clodius, disguised in woman's clothing, at her festival, held in the house of Julius Caesar (who was Pontifex Maximus and whose wife Pompeia was Clodius' mistress).

Boreas

The North Wind, son of the dawn (Eos) and the stars (Astraeus). He was worshipped in Attica because a north wind had assisted the Greeks at the naval battle of Artemisium.

Bori

Father of Bor, who was the father of Odin.

Bors

Sir Bors de Ganis, one of the knights of King Arthur's Round Table and a cousin of Sir LAUNCELOT.

Bragi

Adopted son of Odin. Actual son of the giantess Gunnlod. He was the god of poetry in Norse mythology and was married to Idunn, the goddess who kept the apples of youth.

Brahma

The senior god (with Vishnu and Shiva) in the Vedic triad. Though the creator of the universe, he is rarely worshipped. He is represented as having four arms and seated on a swan. In his hands he holds a sceptre, a string of beads, a bow, and a book of the sacred scriptures.

Branstock

The tree in the Volsung's palace into which Odin thrust a sword. Only Sigmund was able to pull it out.

Briareus (called **Aegaeon** by men)

One of the fifty-headed, hundred-handed monsters *(Hecatoncheires)* born of Heaven and Earth who in the war between the gods and the Titans aided the gods. There were three of them: Cottus, Briareus, and Gyes. In the first book of the *Iliad* there is a curious reference to Briareus. It is said that Hera, Poseidon, and Athena plotted to seize and bind Zeus and (apparently) would have done so had not the nymph Thetis brought Briareus to sit by Zeus as a sort of bodyguard and the very sight of him was so terrifying that "fear crept over those blessed gods and they bound him not."

Briseis

A slave girl, in the *Iliad,* who had been awarded to Achilles and then was taken from him by Agamemnon. This was the cause of "the wrath of Peleus' son" which Homer states as the theme of the epic. Agamemnon was finally persuaded to restore the girl to Achilles.

Brisingamen

Freya's necklace, made by the dwarfs.

Brunhild (also **Brunnehilde, Brynhild**)

In the *Volsung Saga* she is a Valkyrie who is wakened from a magic sleep by Sigurd. She has been put into this sleep by Odin, her father, dooming her to wake and love as a mortal, in punishment for having defended in battle those whom the NORNS had predestined to death. Sigurd later impersonates Gunnar to enable Gunnar to win her. When she discovers what Sigurd has done she has him murdered and then takes her own life.

In the *Nibelungenlied* she is queen of Iceland, who can be won only by one who overcomes her in three trials of strength. Siegfried, by various magical properties, defeats her, enabling Gunther to marry her. She has SIEGFRIED killed by Hagen.

Cacus

A giant son of Vulcan who appears in Roman mythology. He stole some of the cattle of Geryon from Hercules and by dragging them backwards into his cave hoped to elude discovery, since he thought their hoofprints would suggest that they had gone in the opposite direction. But Hercules heard the cattle lowing and killed Cacus.

Cadmus

The son of Agenor, king of Tyre, and the brother of Europa. He founded the town of Thebes and introduced the alphabet into Greece.

Best known of his adventures was his killing of a dragon. On the advice of Athena he sowed the dragon's teeth and from them sprang a crop of armed men whom he destroyed by inciting them to fight one another. Only five survived, to found the nobility of Thebes.

He married Harmonia, the daughter of Ares and Aphrodite. He gave Harmonia a famous necklace made by Hephaestus. Among their children were Ino and Semele. In their old age Cadmus and Harmonia were changed into serpents.

CAENEUS

Caeneus

A Lapith *(see* LAPITHAE*)*. Originally a girl, she was raped by Poseidon, who then offered to grant her a wish. Still possessing at least her virginal indignation, she asked to be changed to a man so that no such experience would befall her again. But, alas, there are burdens in being a man, too. A man, he died in the fight between the Lapithae and the Centaurs at the wedding of Pirithous and Hippodamia (or Deidamia). Other forms of her/his legend state, however, that Caeneus was invulnerable and did not die but merely sank into the earth alive, pressed down under the enormous weight of the rocks and tree trunks which the Centaurs had hurled upon him. That buried under all this, presumably for eternity, he was not dead must be a condition that offers whatever minimum consolation immortality can offer.

Calais and Zetes

Sons of Boreas, the North Wind, they were winged and hence were able to release their brother-in-law PHINEUS from the torment of the HARPIES, which, as punishment for his cruelty, befouled his food so that he could not eat it. They were among the Argonauts and urged the abandonment of Hercules at Cios because he delayed too long searching for Hylas. For this Hercules later killed them.

Calchas

The seer who accompanied the Greek army against Troy. It was he who foretold the necessity of sacrificing Iphigenia and later, at Troy, divined the cause of the plague that had smitten the Greek army. An oracle had foretold that he would die when he met a greater seer than himself, and this he did when he met Mopsus (who told the number of figs on a tree when Calchas could not). Another legend states that he died from laughing when, as he raised a cup of wine to his lips, someone prophesied that he would never live to drink it.

Calliope

The Muse of epic poetry. The mother (by Apollo) of OR-PHEUS.

Calliste

The name under which Artemis was worshipped in Arcadia in the form of a bear.

Callisto

Daughter of LYCAON. Beloved of Zeus, she bore him ARCAS. She was a great huntress, hence under the protection of Artemis. And either that goddess, offended at her unchastity, or Hera, jealous, turned her into a she-bear. In some versions of her legend she was shot by Artemis and in others by her own son. Some accounts say that Zeus transformed her into the constellation of the Great Bear and her son into the star Arcturus (the Bear-watcher).

Calydonian Boar Hunt, The

Oeneus, king of Calydon, in Aetolia, and husband of Althaea, had neglected to pay due honor to the goddess Artemis. In punishment she sent a huge boar to ravage his land. MELEA-GER, his son, called on great hunters to aid him in hunting down the beast, and the list of responding heroes included so many eminent names of the generation immediately preceding that of the *Iliad* that the hunt became, like the story of the Argonauts, a saga in itself. Among those who came to Calydon to hunt the boar were Amphiaraus, Ancaeus, Jason, Nestor, Peleus, Pirithous, Telamon, and Theseus.

CALYPSO

There came also the huntress ATALANTA, who wounded the boar. Meleager killed it and, moved by Atalanta's beauty, gave her its head and hide, the trophies of the hunt. This angered Plexippus and Toxeus, brothers of Queen Althaea. They attacked the maiden and in defending her, Meleager killed them both. Althaea, on hearing of her brothers' death, threw into the fire the half-burned brand on which her son's life depended. As a result, he died and she, remorseful, committed suicide.

Calypso

A nymph, daughter of Atlas, who lived on the lonely island of Ogygia ("the navel of the sea"), onto which the shipwrecked Odysseus was washed ashore after leaving Circe. Odysseus spent seven years with her. She offered him immortality and perpetual youth if he would stay with her but, "sore longing for the sight of the smoke rising from his own hearthstone," he refused, then Zeus sent Hermes to command her to let Odysseus go. Various legends variously attribute three sons to this sojourn: Auson, Nausithous, and Nausinous.

Camelot

The place of King Arthur's court. Malory says it was Winchester but other places claim the honor.

Camilla

A Volscian maiden, a virgin huntress and warrior, dear to the goddess Diana. She was so light of foot that she scarcely bent the stalks as she hurried over the fields of grain and she skimmed dry-foot over the surface of the water ["swift Camilla:" who "scours the plain/ Flies o'er th' unbending corn, and skims along the main"—Alexander Pope]. She was killed in battle by the Etruscan Arruns—who was himself soon thereafter dispatched by the arrows of the sorrowing goddess.

Most notable incident in her life was her being fastened to a spear by her father, Metabus, and thrown across the Amisenus river, in order to escape their pursuing enemies.

Capaneus

See SEVEN AGAINST THEBES.

Carthage

A city on the coast of Africa, opposite Sicily. It was founded by Dido, daughter of Belus, king of Tyre. After the death of her father, her brother, Pygmalion, had her wealthy husband, Sichaeus, killed and Dido fled from Tyre. Arriving at the site of her future city, she asked the natives for as much land as could be enclosed with a bull's hide. The request granted, she had a bull's hide cut into narrow strips and with them she enclosed a space which became the city.

See also DIDO, AENEAS.

Cassandra (also called **Alexandra**)

Daughter of Priam, king of Troy. The god Apollo, to win her love, gave her the gift of prophecy. But when she refused his advances he nullified the gift (which it was not in his power to recall) by decreeing that no one would ever believe her prophecies. She warned her countrymen against the Wooden Horse, for example, but her warning went unheeded. At the sack of Troy she became the slave of Agamemnon and on his return to Argos was killed with him by Clytemnestra.

Cassiopeia

Wife of Cepheus, king of the Aethiopians. She foolishly boasted that she was more beautiful than the NEREIDS, and

CASTALIA

Poseidon, to punish her presumption, sent a sea monster to ravage the coast of her father's kingdom. An oracle stated that the monster could be appeased and the country saved only if the couple's daughter ANDROMEDA were chained to a rock and offered to the monster. She was saved from death, however, by Perseus, and the boastful mother was set in the constellation called Cassiopeia's Chair.

[Milton, in *Il Penseroso*, refers to:

> That starred Aethiope queen that strove
> To set her beauty's praise above
> The sea-nymphs, and their powers offended.]

Castalia

Spring or fountain at the foot of Parnassus. It was sacred to the Muses. In it Pythia, the priestess of the Delphic oracle, bathed and/or drank for inspiration.

Castor and Pollux (or Polydeuces), the Dioscuri

They are the brothers of Helen. Twins (hatched from one egg) though they are and both sons of Leda, Castor was the son of Tyndareus and Polydeuces (*Pollux* being the Roman name) of Zeus. When Castor was killed (in a fight with the brothers of Phoebe and Hilaeira, maidens whom the twins had carried off), Pollux, who was immortal, asked Zeus to be allowed to share his immortality with his brother. The request was granted and they spend alternate days in Hades and on Olympus.

[They are usually identified with the constellation of Gemini and their ghosts hover, faint and far-off, in our common exclamation of "By Jiminy!"]

Cecrops

The founder and first king of Athens. Below the waist he was shaped like a serpent. He was thought to have introduced monogamy, funerals, and the alphabet.

Celeus

An old man of Eleusis who had hospitably received DEMETER when she was wandering, distraught, in search of PERSEPHONE. In gratitude Demeter restored Celeus' son, Triptolemus, to health as he lay dying and later taught him the use of the plow and other secrets of agriculture. He built a temple to her in Eleusis and established her worship in the Eleusinian Mysteries.

Centaurs

Mythical beasts having the upper part of a human being and the lower part of a horse, or a human head and torso rising from the chest and shoulders of a horse. They were lustful, bibulous, and aggressive. One legend of their origin is that they were born of Ixion, king of the Lapithae, and a cloud which Zeus had sent to him in the form of Hera, Ixion having boasted of receiving favors from Hera. The Centaurs were eventually driven out by the Lapithae after a battle ensuing upon the Centaurs' rowdy misbehavior at a wedding.

See NESSUS, CHIRON.

Cephalus

The husband of Procris. He tested her chastity by staying away eight years—during which time he was abducted by Eos, the dawn, who wooed him in vain. He came back in disguise and seduced Procris, just to test her love—he having remained faithful to her in his heart throughout his long absence. She followed him secretly when he went hunting and was killed accidentally when he mistook her for a wild animal.

Cerberus

The three-headed dog that guarded the entrance to the lower world. The creature was conceived of as having a serpent's tail and a mane of serpents. One of the labors of Hercules was to drag this formidable monster up into the upper world and after showing it to Eurystheus (who had set the Twelve Labors) to take it back. The Greeks buried with a corpse a cake of honey wherewith the spirit could mollify Cerberus— hence "a sop to Cerberus."

Ceres

An Italian goddess of grain identified with DEMETER.

Cerynean Stag

As his third or fourth labor (the order of the performance of his feats differs in different accounts) Hercules was required to bring Eurystheus one of the wonderful deer with antlers of gold and hooves of brass that ranged the hills of Cerynea. In various accounts the creature actually captured is called a stag or a hind. Since they had antlers, even if of gold, they would seem to have been stags. But they were magic, and unimpeachable authorities say they were hinds.

The most important thing about them was that they were sacred to Artemis and if Hercules harmed one of them he would incur the wrath of the goddess. But he met the difficulty by stalking one of the creatures for a whole year until he was able to get close enough to hobble its front legs and catch it without injuring it. He then carried it carefully to Eurystheus.

Cestus

The embroidered girdle of Aphrodite which conferred upon the wearer irresistible charm.

[In no way to be confused with the Roman *cestus,* the leather glove studded with iron spikes which the Roman boxers used. *Its* charm was considerably less than irresistible.]

Ceto

A goddess of the sea, daughter of Gaea and Pontus and the sister and wife of Phorcys. She was the mother of the Gorgons, of Scylla, and of Ladon, the serpent-dragon that guarded the Golden Apples of the Hesperides.

Ceyx

The husband of *Alcyone.* They were turned into kingfishers as punishment for referring to themselves as Zeus and Hera. Another version, however, states that he was drowned and she leaped into the sea to die with him and the pitying gods turned them into kingfishers.

Chaos

According to Hesiod, the first thing that "came into being."

Charis

The personification of grace and beauty, she was the wife of Hephaestus. In other accounts there were three Charites, daughters of Zeus and attendants upon Aphrodite. The Romans identified them with the Graces.

Charon

The old, bad-tempered ferryman who ferried the spirits of the dead across the river Styx into the underworld. There was a small charge for the service and the Greeks used to put a coin in the mouth of the dead to pay Charon his fare.

Charybdis

The dreaded whirlpool that guards one side of a narrow channel (in the *Odyssey;* later, but groundlessly, assumed to be the Straits of Messina) whose other side is guarded by the monster Scylla. Circe warns Odysseus, who must pass the channel, that he will not survive Charybdis and so must take his chance with Scylla. The two are used jointly as an expression for frightful or distressing alternatives, one of which *must* be selected.

Chemosh

The principal god of the Moabites. Mentioned in the Old Testament (I Kings 11; II Kings 23). Characterized as "the obscene dread of Moab's sons," he appears in *Paradise Lost* (I, 406) as one of the fallen angels.

Chimera

A fire-breathing monster whose body consisted of a lion in front, a goat in the middle, and a serpent behind. It was killed by Bellerophon.

   [Even in the fantasies of mythology it was felt to be extreme and the word today suggests something absurdly fantastic, wildly imaginary.]

Chiron

A Centaur, son of Cronus and an Oceanid. Though most Centaurs were wild and quarrelsome and violently destructive, Chiron was a friend to man, wise and skilled in hunting, music, and medicine. He was the tutor of Aesculapius, of Jason, Hercules, and Achilles. During Hercules' fight with the Centaurs, Chiron (an old friend of Hercules') was accidentally struck by one of Hercules' poisoned arrows. Since he was immortal, this would mean never-ending pain and he asked to die. Zeus placed him among the stars, where he is Sagittarius, the archer. Some accounts say that he surrendered his immortality to Prometheus.

Chryseis

Daughter of a priest of Apollo, she is taken prisoner and given to Agamemnon. Her father attempts to ransom her but Agamemnon refuses to give her up and Apollo sends a plague on the Greek army. To placate the god the maiden is returned but Agamemnon demands, in compensation, that he be given the maid Briseis, who had been given to Achilles. Thus began the fateful quarrel that shaped so much of the action of the *Iliad*.

Chryses

A priest of Apollo who appears in the *Iliad*. His daughter, Chryseis, had been captured by the Greeks and given to Agamemnon. Chryses came to the Greek camp to beg for his daughter but was rudely dismissed and Apollo, offended at this slight to his priest, sent a plague to scourge the Grecian camp. CALCHAS, the seer, revealed the cause of the plague and said that the maiden must be returned to her father. Agamemnon, after much angry blustering, consented to give up the girl only if he were given Briseis, a maiden assigned to Achilles. This aroused the wrath of Achilles which, we are told in the first line of the poem, is the theme of the epic.

Cimmerians

A mythical people who are described in Homer as living in a land of perpetual darkness. Not to be confused with an actual

CINYRAS

people who in antiquity inhabited the north shore of the Black Sea, between the Danube and the Don.

Cinyras

The mythical founder of the cult of Aphrodite in Cyprus—with which her worship was so firmly connected that she was often called the *Cyprian Aphrodite* or simply the *Cyprian*. Cinyras was the father of Adonis by unwitting incest with his daughter, Myrrha.

Circe

An enchantress who lived on the island of Aeaea. She was the daughter of Helios, the sister of Aeëtes, and the aunt of Medea. Odysseus and his men landed on her island. She changed the men into swine but Odysseus (with help from Hermes, who was sent by the gods to give him a sprig of the magic herb moly) resisted her spells and compelled her to free his men and restore them to their human shapes. He stayed with her long enough to beget three sons, Agrius, LATINUS, and TELEGONIS. It was at Circe's suggestion, when he left, that he went to the underworld to consult Tiresias.

Clashing Rocks (or Wandering Rocks)

See SYMPLEGADES.

Cleobis and Biton

Sons of the priestess of Hera at Argos. When the oxen that were to draw the sacred chariot in the goddess' rites did not arrive, the young men dragged the chariot themselves for several miles. Delighted with such muscular piety, the priestess besought the goddess to give them the finest gift she could bestow on mortals—and they both immediately fell asleep and died quietly in their sleep.

Clio

The Muse of history.

Clotho

One of the Fates *(see* MOERAE), she who spins the thread of life.

Clymene

A Titaness, the daughter of Oceanus and Tethys and the wife of IAPETUS, to whom she bore PROMETHEUS, EPIMETHEUS, and ATLAS.

Clytemnestra

The daughter of Tyndareus and Leda. She was sister to Castor and half sister to Helen and Pollux. She was the wife of Agamemnon, the mother of Orestes, Electra, Iphigenia, and Chrysothemis. And she was the paramour of Aegisthus. On her husband's return from Troy she murdered him—partly (according to various forms of her legend) out of hatred for his sacrifice of Iphigenia and partly out of jealousy of Cassandra, whom he had brought back as a captive concubine. In retaliation for the murder of Agamemnon, she was killed by her son Orestes.

Clytie

A water nymph in love with Apollo. In some versions of the legend he at first returned her love and then deserted her for Leucothea, but in other versions he was simply indifferent to her. For days she sat desolate, following with her eyes the sun on his journey until the sun god changed her into a heliotrope, or sunflower.

CNOSSUS

Cnossus (or Cnosus, Gnossus)

The ancient capital of Crete, home of King Minos.

Cocytus

The river of lamentation, one of the five rivers of the underworld in Greek mythology.

Coeus

A Titan, father of Leto by Phoebe.

Coronis

Daughter of Phlegyas, she bore Aesculapius to Apollo. But while pregnant with Aesculapius she had an affair with Ischys, an Arcadian. A crow carried the news to Apollo, who had Artemis kill her but took the unborn child from her body on the funeral pyre and gave it to Chiron to be cared for and educated.

Corybantes

Priests who led the worship of Rhea, especially under her name of Cybele, the Mighty Mother. Her worship was characterized by percussion music and orgiastic dancing.

Cranes of Ibycus, The

See Ibycus.

Creon

1. Son of Menoeceus and king of Thebes. He was the brother of Jocasta and offered her hand, after the death of Laius to anyone who would rid the kingdom of the Sphinx. After Oedipus was driven out, Creon assumed the kingship. During the attack of the Seven Against Thebes he refused burial to Poly-

nices *(see* ANTIGONE). His son Haemon killed himself over the body of Antigone, his betrothed, and another son, Menoeceus, killed himself as a sacrifice to expiate the guilt incurred by all Thebes as a consequence of Cadmus' killing of the dragon *(see* MENOECEUS).

2. King of Corinth, whose daughter GLAUCE, about to marry Jason, was killed by a poisonous garment treacherously given to her by MEDEA.

Cretan Bull

Poseidon gave MINOS, king of Crete, a magnificent bull to sacrifice. But MINOS so admired the creature that he did not sacrifice it and Poseidon, angry, drove the bull mad, so that it terrorized the countryside. As his seventh labor Hercules captured the bull, brought it back to Mycenae and sacrificed it to Hera.

Whether this was the bull that fathered the MINOTAUR or whether it was the bull that carried EUROPA to Crete differs in various forms of the legend.

Creusa

1. Daughter of Erechtheus, king of Athens. She was raped by Apollo and bore a son. The child was exposed to die but was taken to Delphi by Hermes and there brought up. Xuthus, Creusa's husband, thought the child his own and brought him back to Athens, calling him *Ion*.

2. First wife of Aeneas and mother of Ascanius. She was killed while trying to escape from burning Troy. Her ghost appeared to Aeneas and warned him of perils to come.

Cronus (or **Cronos, Kronos**)

A Titan, son of Uranus and Gaea (or Ge). He emasculated his father and seized control of the world. By his consort Rhea he begot the Olympians: ZEUS, POSEIDON, HADES, HERA, HESTIA, and DEMETER. It having been foretold that he would be overthrown by one of his children, he swallowed them—all except Zeus, the last-born, for whom Rhea substituted a stone in swaddling clothes, having the actual Zeus reared in a secret cave on the island of Crete and suckled by a she-goat. After he had defeated his father, Zeus made him vomit up the other Olympians.

Ctesippus

One of the insolent suitors in the *Odyssey*. He hurled a bone at the disguised Odysseus.

Cuchulain

One of the greatest warriors of Celtic mythology. Possibly son of the sun god. His name was etymologized to mean "the hound of Culain," the story being that having killed the dog of one Culain he was remorseful and offered to serve as Culain's watchdog until Culain could find another as good as the one killed.

One segment of his saga has to do with his killing in battle his heroic son Conlaoch, whom he did not know to be his son. Cuchulain is finally slain in battle.

Cumaean Sibyl

See SIBYL(S).

Cupid

The "blind bow boy" to which the Romans reduced the Greek Eros.

See EROS and also PSYCHE.

Curetes

Those supernatural figures, resembling armed men, who protected the infant Zeus in Crete, drowning out his cries by clashing cymbals and their shields so that he would not be discovered by his father, Cronus.

Cybele (also called **Rhea**)

The wife of Cronus and hence mother of the Olympian gods. Her priests were called *Corybantes* and her rites were celebrated with wild orgies. Sacred to her were the oak, the pine, and the lion. She was usually represented as being drawn in a chariot by lions, with a crown on her head and a small drum or cymbal in her hand.

Cyclops (or **Cyclopes**)

Gigantic, one-eyed creatures. In the *Odyssey* they are ferocious pastoral giants, given to cannibalism. Polyphemus, their leader, is a son of Poseidon and when Odysseus blinds him, that he and his surviving men may escape from the giant's cave, Poseidon (in answer to his son's prayer for vengeance) pursues Odysseus with undying hatred.

In Hesiod, however, the Cyclops are the sons of Uranus and Gaea. There are three of them: Brontes, Steropes, and Arges. They help Zeus in his war against Cronus, and it is they who fashioned his thunderbolts. In later legends they are (1) slain by Apollo or (2) reduced to being workmen for Hephaestus.

Cycnus (= "swan")

1. Son of Apollo by Thyria. Mother and son leaped into Lake Canope and were both changed into swans.

CYNTHIA

2. Son of Poseidon. He was king of Colonae in Troas and was killed by Achilles. He was changed into a swan.

3. A ruffian son of Ares who robbed those who brought gifts to the shrine of Apollo at Delphi. He was slain by Hercules, who, in the fighting, wounded Ares himself. He was changed into a swan.

4. A friend of PHAËTHON. While lamenting Phaëthon's death he was changed into a swan by Apollo and placed among the stars.

Cynthia

The goddess ARTEMIS was sometimes called *Cynthia* because she was born on Mount Cynthus on Delos.

Cytherea

The goddess APHRODITE was sometimes called *Cytherea* because it was near the island Cythera that she rose from the sea-foam.

Daedalus

An Athenian, descendant of Erechtheus, famed as a cunning artificer. He fled from Athens to Crete after killing his nephew Perdix, of whose skills—similar to his own—he was jealous. At Crete, in the service of King Minos and Queen Pasiphaë, he constructed the bronze cow which permitted the queen to gratify her strange lust and the Labyrinth to house the Minotaur that resulted from it. In some versions of his story it was he who devised the clew which Ariadne gave to Theseus to enable him to escape from the Labyrinth.

Daedalus was imprisoned by Minos and escaped by constructing wings for himself and his son Icarus. Despite his father's warning the boy flew too close to the sun, the wax in his artificial wings melted, and he fell into the sea and was drowned. Daedalus, however, got safely to Sicily.

Daemon

A spirit assigned to each individual by Zeus to watch over him throughout his life. The Roman equivalent was a *Genius.*

[In English *daemon* is still sometimes used by the highly literate to indicate an indwelling, motivating spirit. But such a use borders on the affected and, spelled *demon,* the word commonly designates an evil spirit. *Genius* kept its older

DAGON

meaning much longer. When Milton, in 1637, apostrophizing his drowned friend, Edward King, says

> Henceforth thou art the Genius of the shore,
> In thy large recompense, and shalt be good
> To all that wander in that perilous flood,

he plainly implied that King was to be a beneficent guardian spirit. Its present meaning of a native inborn power or ability of an exalted kind is comparatively recent. Johnson did not recognize it in his *Dictionary* (1755).]

Dagon

The fish god of the Philistines, worshipped especially in Gaza and Ashdod. Samson died in a temple of Dagon. The Ark was desecrated by being placed in the temple of Dagon at Ashdod and the idol worshipped there was tumbled and broken (I Samuel 5). The head of the slain Saul was fastened as a trophy in the temple of Dagon at Beth-shan.

Damocles

Friend of Dionysius, the tyrant of Syracuse. On his expressing envy of the tyrant's felicity, Dionysius invited him to try it. He was seated at a sumptuous table, with all known delicacies before him. But over his head a sword was suspended by a single hair and the envied banquet proved to be an unenviable torment.

[Though very old, this, of course, is a moral story, not a myth. It is but a dramatization of the thought in Shakespeare's "Uneasy lies the head that wears a crown." But the converse, which Shakespeare develops, that the "happy low" lie down in restful peace, is unwarranted.]

Danaë

Daughter of Acrisius, king of Argos. Her father, forewarned
that she would bear a child that would kill him, shut her up in
a tower, but Zeus visited her there, in the form of a shower
of gold, and she bore the hero Perseus. When her father
learned of this he set mother and infant afloat in a chest. The
chest was carried to the island of Seriphus, where they were
received by the king, Polydectes. Later, however, Polydectes
became jealous or fearful of PERSEUS and sent him to obtain
the head of the Gorgon Medusa. He succeeded in the quest
and, returning, exposed the head and turned Polydectes to
stone.

Danaïdes

See AEGYPTUS.

Danaus

King of Argos, twin brother of AEGYPTUS and father of the
fifty Danaïdes.

Daphne

The daughter of a river god. She was desired by Apollo but
fled as he pursued her and (in answer to her prayer to Zeus)
was changed into a laurel.

Daphnis

A shepherd who was blinded by a nymph when he was unfaithful to her. In his blindness he consoled himself with pastoral music, of which he was the inventor. Another version of
the story states that he loved no one and Aphrodite, piqued
by this questioning of her omnipotence, inspired in him a
passionate love. But rather than yield to it he died. Some

versions say that Pan taught him to sing and play the lyre and that the nymph Piplea loved him but was jealous and turned him into a stone.

[*Daphnis and Chloe* is a sentimental prose romance written in the fourth century A.D. by Longus (of whom nothing but the authorship of this tale is known). It has been much reworked, being the basis, for instance, of Allan Ramsay's *Gentle Shepherd.* It affected Amyot and Tasso and its retelling by Bernadin de St. Pierre, in 1788, as *Paul and Virginia,* had a strong effect on the romantic poets.]

Dardanus

Son of Zeus and the Pleiad Electra, he was the father of ERICHTHONIUS and the founder of Troy.

Deianira (or **Dejaneira**)

Daughter of Oeneus, sister of Meleager, and wife of Hercules, who won her by defeating Achelous. As the Centaur Nessus was carrying her across a river he attempted to violate her and Hercules shot him with a poisoned arrow. The dying Centaur told Deianira to preserve some of his blood, assuring her that it would recall Hercules' love should it ever stray. When, years later, Hercules brought Iole home from Oechalia, Deianira soaked a garment in the blood and sent it to him as a gift. When he put the garment on it burned his flesh and could not be removed, so that he died in agony. Deianira killed herself in remorse.

See also LICHAS.

Deiphobus

One of the sons of Priam who fought against the Greeks at Troy. After Paris' death he married Helen but was slain by

Menelaus. He appears in Shakespeare's *Troilus and Cressida.*

Deirdre

Sometimes called *Deirdre of the Sorrows.* Daughter of a bard at the court of Ulster, in Celtic legendry. Conchobar, king of Ulster, intended to marry her, but she ran away with Naoise. Later he and his brothers were killed and Deirdre died of grief.

Delos

The island (formerly called *Ortygia)* on which the goddess LETO found sanctuary, when pregnant by Zeus, from the pursuing hatred of Hera. And there she gave birth to her great twin children, Apollo and Artemis. The island was a floating island but after this event it became fixed.

Demeter

The goddess of vegetation and fruitfulness. Daughter of Cronus and Rhea and hence one of the Olympians. In various myths she had various consorts—Zeus and Poseidon among them. One legend concerned her lying in the furrowed field with (or being attacked by) Iasion, whom Zeus slew with a thunderbolt.

Her most important myth concerns her relations with her daughter Persephone, who was carried off by Hades. Demeter sought her daughter over the face of the earth, while all vegetation and fruits withered. Zeus, that men should not all die of starvation, had Persephone returned to her but, because Persephone had eaten six pomegranate seeds while in the underworld she could not return permanently but was allowed to spend six months in the upper world and six months in the underworld. All of this is plainly connected with the vegetative cycle and was, apparently, a part of the Eleusinian Mysteries.

Another legend concerns the child of Celeus, king of Eleusis, into whose house Demeter, in her wanderings, was taken as a nurse, her real identity being unknown. She intended to confer immortality upon the child and every night placed it in the fire to burn away some of its mortality but was surprised by Metanira, Celeus' wife, who indignantly put a stop to the process.

Demodocus

The blind minstrel who, at the court of Alcinous, king of the Phaeacians, sings songs about the Trojan War and makes (the as-yet-unrevealed) Odysseus weep.

Demogorgon

Attending the thrones of Chaos and his consort, sable-vested Night, Milton's Satan, in his great flight through space, finds "Orcus and Ades, and the dreaded name of Demogorgon." ORCUS we know was a vague and menacing monster of enormous size. Ades is simply Hades. But who or what is Demogorgon?

Statius (first century A.D.) in his epic poem *Thebaid* (IV, 514) mentions a "Most High One," a god so dreadful that it is unlawful to even know he exists. This, naturally, aroused a certain amount of eerie speculation and this was, presumably, satisfied by a revelation by Lactantius (c. 250 A.D.) that this being's name was *Demogorgon*. And later still, some medieval thinkers were of the opinion that this was Satan's actual name (dreaded because spirits and their names were closely connected and a mention of the name might produce the spirit). But H. J. Rose believes it was simply "a copyist's blunder for Demiurgus, i.e., the Creator."]

DEUCALION AND PYRRHA

Demophon

A son of Theseus, with whom the Thracian maiden Phyllis fell in love. He left Thrace for Athens, promising to return. But he was long delayed and in despair she hanged herself. After her death she was changed into an almond tree and when he finally returned and, hearing of her fate, embraced the tree, it came into leaf.

Another story is told—that Demophon married Phyllis and then tired of her. She gave him a mysterious box which he was to open only if he definitely decided he did not love her any more. He was away so long that she, in despair, cursed him, took poison, and died. In that very hour he opened the box. What he saw therein is not known, but the sight of it drove him raving mad. He fell from his horse on his own sword and was killed.

Deucalion and **Pyrrha**

Deucalion, the "Noah" of Greek mythology, was the son of Prometheus, and his wife Pyrrha was the daughter of Epimetheus. Warned that Zeus intended to flood the earth because of men's wickedness, he built a chest in which he and his wife floated for nine days, landing at last on Mount Parnassus. Ordered to veil their faces and throw behind them "the bones of their mother," they interpreted this to refer to mother earth and threw stones over their shoulders as they walked. Those thrown by Deucalion turned into men, those thrown by Pyrrha into women. And the earth was repopulated.

DIANA

Diana

An ancient Roman goddess of the moon, a virgin and a huntress and a helper of females in childbirth. All of this made it natural for her to be identified with ARTEMIS.

Dice (or Dike)

One of the HORAE. She was a personification of justice and reported to Zeus the evil that men did. In this capacity she was sometimes called *Astraea*.

Dido

Queen of Carthage. She fell in love with Aeneas, who had been driven by a storm upon her shores. When, in obedience to a command of the gods, he left her, she burned herself to death on a funeral pyre. Later when Aeneas, visiting the underworld, saw her and attempted to speak to her, she spurned him.

[Matthew Arnold in *The Scholar-Gipsy* urges the truant scholar to

> Fly hence, our contact fear!
> Still fly, plunge deeper in the bowering wood!
> Averse, as Dido did with gesture stern
> From her false friend's approach in Hades turn,
> Wave us away, and keep thy solitude!]

Diomedes

1. A Thracian king, son of Ares. He owned some ferocious, flesh-eating horses, the capture of which was one of Hercules' Twelve Labors. Hercules not only captured the horses but fed Diomedes to them.

2. Son of Tydeus and king of Argos. One of the greatest of

the Greek warriors in the fight against Troy. He fought personal combats with Hector and Aeneas. He wounded the god Ares himself "in the nethermost belly" so that Ares ran bellowing to Zeus. He also wounded Aphrodite—who wept but did not bellow and caused his wife to love another and desert him. He and Odysseus stole the Palladium from Troy, thus ensuring the city's fall. One of the more famous incidents in his career was his exchanging armor with GLAUCUS.

[Diomedes became a figure in poetry and drama through the ages by being the man who displaced Troilus in the affections of Crysede, or Cressida. But this (though a Troilus is mentioned in the *Iliad)* is a medieval, not an ancient, legend.]

Dione

A Titaness. In some accounts she is the mother, by Zeus, of Aphrodite—though in the better-known account Aphrodite is born of the sea-foam. Dione is sometimes used as a name for Aphrodite herself.

Dionysus

Son of Zeus and Semele. His mother, tricked by jealous Hera, demanded that her divine lover come to her in his true state and, since Zeus was the god of lightning, she was consumed to ashes. From her charred remains, however, Zeus took the unborn child and sewed it up within his own thigh until it reached maturity.

Dionysus was a fertility god, especially in regard to the vine, but he was not, like his Roman counterpart Bacchus, solely a god of wine. He was a freer of emotions, a remover of inhibitions. The celebration of his rites was marked by the wild frenzy of his female devotees. It was they—Maenads, Bacchantes, Bassarides—that tore to pieces PENTHEUS and

DIOSCURI

ORPHEUS. From some of the stylized dances of these rites and their songs grew the drama.

Dioscuri (= "the sons of Zeus")

See CASTOR AND POLLUX.

Dirce

The woman for whom Lycus abandoned his first wife, ANTIOPE. She mistreated Antiope and Antiope's sons, Amphion and Zethus, bound her to the horns of a wild bull and had her dragged to death.

Dis

See HADES.

Discordia

The Roman name for the Greek ERIS.

Djinn

Spirits in Mohammedan mythology, lower than the angels and influencing men for good or evil. They are capable of appearing in human or animal form. *Djinn* (or *Jinn)* is the plural form, the singular being *Djinni* or *Jinni.*

Influenced by the old English meaning of *genius* as a spirit ("Henceforth thou art the genius of the shore"), the word is often spelled *genie,* though this is usually treated as a singular.

Dolius

The "age-crippled herdsman" who with his sons stood ready to fight and die for Odysseus as the enraged kinsmen of the dead suitors advanced upon him.

Dolon

In a night reconnaissance into the Trojan lines, Odysseus and Diomedes capture Dolon, a Trojan spy who has been sent by Hector to reconnoiter the Grecian camp. He begs for his life. Odysseus encourages him to believe that they will merely take him prisoner. But Diomedes, after they have gained what information they can from him, kills him.

Draupnir

The magic ring or armlet made for Odin by the dwarf Sindri. Eight duplicate bracelets fell from it every ninth night. It was placed on Balder's funeral pyre. Balder, in Hel, gave it to Hermod to take back to Odin.

Dryope

A nymph who, deceived, had a son, Amphissus, by Apollo. She was turned into a poplar, or at least a poplar was made to appear where she was last seen.

Dwarfs

Diminutive supernatural creatures in Norse mythology who sprang from the decaying body of YIR. They live underground and are skillful in magic workmanship. They killed the wise man Kvasir, from whose blood Odin made Odhaerir, the mead of poetic inspiration. They also made the chain GLEIPNIR with which Fenrir, the wolf monster, is bound.

Dynadin

A knight in Malory's *Morte d'Arthur* who seems intended to be humorous. But the intention is so faint, the execution so slight and the whole idea so unexpected and unusual in that work, that one is not quite certain. He often speaks with dry common sense which, in itself, constitutes a ludicrous intrusion into the wild romanticism of chivalry and courtly love. At one time we are told that he composed a song mocking King Mark of Cornwall (who is represented throughout the story as a contemptible man) and at another time that he scoffs at lovers. Then he frequently gets buffeted by mistake.

[Sir Dynadin had a brief afterglow of literary immortality when he appeared as Sir Dinadan the Humorist in Mark Twain's *A Connecticut Yankee in King Arthur's Court* (Chapter IV).]

Echidna

A monster and a prolific breeder of monsters. Half-woman, half-serpent, her parentage is variously given as Tartarus and Gaea, Phorcys and Ceto, or Chrysaor and Callirrhoë. By Typhon she bore the Chimera, Cerberus, and the Lernean Hydra. She bore Geryon's hound, the two-headed dog Orthros, and by Orthros she bore the Sphinx and the Nemean Lion. An end was put to this foul fecundity by Argus, who killed her while she slept.

[A large part of Hercules' labors seems to have consisted of cleaning up after Echidna! *See* HERCULES.]

Echo

There are two stories of Echo. The grimmer one is that Pan desired her but she fled his advances and he, to be revenged, had her torn to pieces by shepherds whom he had driven mad—torn so completely to pieces that only a fragment of her voice survived.

A more delightful explanation is that she was attendant upon the goddess Hera but chattered so much that Zeus could always hear his wife and her train as they approached and hence had time to conceal whatever amour he was engaged in. Hera, to silence the nymph, denied her the power of speech, except to repeat what others said. She pined away to nothing but an answering voice.

See also NARCISSUS.

Ector

1. Sir Ector, to whom, in Malory's *Morte d'Arthur,* the infant Arthur was entrusted. He was the father of Sir Kay, the seneschal.

2. Sir Ector de Maris, also in Malory and a knight of the Round Table. He was the brother of Sir Launcelot, over whose corpse he uttered a famous lament.

Eddas

The *Eddas* are the books that serve as the sources for what we know of Norse mythology. The chief *Eddas* are the Codex Regius (*c.* 1090) and the *Prose Edda* (*c.* 1220) compiled by Snorri Sturluson. Both were discovered in Iceland.

Egeria

A water nymph who, in Roman mythology, advised Numa, the second king of Rome (seventh century B.C.), especially concerning religious rites.

Eidothea

A sea nymph who took pity on Menelaus, becalmed on his return from Troy to Sparta, and advised him to lie in wait for her father PROTEUS, who could be compelled to give him useful advice and information if Menelaus would only seize him and hold on to him, unafraid. This was not a simple matter, since Proteus had the power to change himself into many and fearsome shapes; but, forewarned, Menelaus held on and got the information he wanted.

Eileithyia

The Greek goddess of childbirth, daughter of Zeus and Hera. A cave in Crete was sacred to her.

Eirene (Irene)

One of the HORAE.
  See also PAX.

Elaine

A common name in Malory's *Morte d'Arthur:*

(1) Daughter of Sir Bernard of Astolat, called "The Lily Maid of Astolat." She died for love of Sir Launcelot.
(2) Daughter of King Pelles and the mother (by Sir Launcelot) of GALAHAD.
(3) Wife of King Nentres.
(4) Wife of King Ban.
(5) Daughter of King Pellanor.

Electra

1. An Oceanid, daughter of Oceanus and Tethys.
2. Mother (by Thaumas) of IRIS, goddess of the rainbow and also of the loathsome HARPIES.
  [It is astonishing, even in mythology, that one mother should produce such different offspring!]
3. The daughter of Agamemnon and Clytemnestra and the sister of Iphigenia, Chrysothemis, and Orestes. Devoted to the memory of her father, she hates her mother and urges on her brother to matricide.
  [She has the distinction of being the central figure in plays by Aeschylus, Sophocles, Euripides, Alfieri, Voltaire,

ELLE

Hofmannsthal, and Eugene O'Neill, and in an opera by Richard Strauss. Only Amphitryon rivals her in this respect!]
4. Daughter of Atlas, one of the Pleiads. By Zeus she was the mother of Dardanus, founder of the royal house of Troy.

[Dante mentions her in the fourth canto of the *Inferno*.]

Elle

Old Age, in the form of an aged hag, with whom Thor wrestled (ingloriously) in the hall of UTGARD-LOKI.

Elpenor

A member of Odysseus' crew who died on Circe's island. He was asleep, drunk, on Circe's roof when he heard the others leaving and in his haste to join them missed the ladder and fell and broke his neck. His was the first ghost to encounter Odysseus in the underworld. He piteously begged for the proper burial that had been denied him in the haste of their departure and Odysseus promised him that he would return to Aeaea and perform the due rites. And he kept his word.

[The incident—aside from its interesting individualization of Odysseus' largely anonymous crew—strengthens our evaluation of the hero's character. It is humane. But it is more; a strong indication to the Greek hearer of the saga of Odysseus' wisdom was his observance of all religious rites and dues. Then, as a good commander he owed his men protection and any Greek would have regarded decent burial as his due, his protection even in death. We see also the strength of Odysseus' character: moved as he was by Elpenor's unhappy fate, and sincere as was his own self-reproach for not having given the wretched man his due rites, he refused to allow him to sip the blood which would enable him to be more alive and feel and speak more vigorously. *That* had to be reserved for those who could help him or out-ranked Elpenor.]

Elysium (or **The Elysian Fields**)

Identified by the Greeks with the Islands of the Blest, a place where all are happy ("resting weary limbs at last on beds of asphodel"), it is sometimes spoken of as if it were a part of the underworld and at other times as if it were quite apart from Hades.

Like the Order of the Garter in Lord Melbourne's estimation, the Elysian Fields had no nonsensical connection with moral merit; those who went there went through the favor of the gods or by having the proper connections. Menelaus, for example, is promised an afterlife in Elysium simply because, being married to Helen, he is Zeus' son-in-law.

Despite the bliss presumably experienced there, one of the very few direct reports we have of Elysium is negative. Odysseus, when he went down into the underworld to seek advice from Tiresias, saw Achilles, who told him that he would rather be a slave of the poorest peasant alive than rule over the dead. He may, however, have had personal reasons for this startling comparison: after death he had married Medea—or she had married him.

Empusae

Monsters, in various frightful forms, sent by Hecate to frighten travelers. They were amorous and generally finished their amours by eating their lovers. Among the Empusae were the Lamiae.

See LAMIA.

ENCELADUS

Enceladus

One of the giants that sprang from the blood of the mutilated URANUS. He had the head and torso of a man but vast, coiling serpents for legs and feet. In the war between the giants and the gods he was buried under Aetna when Athena hurled all of Sicily at him.

Endymion

A beautiful young man, a shepherd on Mount Latmos, who was loved by the moon. He lies in eternal sleep. One version states that he asked this somnolence of Zeus as a means of remaining forever young. Another version states that Selene (the moon) herself put him to sleep that she might visit him in full quiet. Still another legend (somewhat incompatible with the preceding!) states that she bore him fifty daughters. These are thought by some scholars to be symbolic of the fifty lunar months between Olympic Games. One version of the legend has Endymion buried at Olympia.

[Keats published a long poem in four books in 1818 using the story of Endymion and weaving into it various other of the Greek legends. Keats himself described the poem as "a feverish attempt rather than a deed accomplished." It was savagely attacked in the reviews.]

Enyo

1. One of the GRAIAE.
2. The goddess of war, in Roman mythology called *Bellona*. Sometimes the wife, sometimes the sister of Ares (who was sometimes called *Enyalios)*. She was distinguished, as the goddess of war, from Athena, the warrior goddess of wisdom, by her ferocity and fury. She rushed madly about the

battlefield with a whip in her hand, lashing the combatants to murderous hatred.

[Today she might be regarded as the goddess of patriotism, of morale, of esprit de corps, of gung-ho.]

Eos (Roman **Aurora**)

The dawn. She was the daughter of Hyperion and Thea. She was the sister of Helios and Selene, and the wife of Astraeus and the mother of Memnon. She had many lovers, among them Clitus, Cephalus, Orion, and Tithonus. Orion, a giant, was killed by Artemis. Eos begged Zeus to make Tithonus, whom she loved, immortal but forgot to ask for eternal youth for him, so that he withered and shrivelled with old age and became completely helpless except for his ceaseless talking, an old man's shrill chirping, which led to his being changed into a cicada.

[One of Tennyson's finest poems consists of a short monologue by Tithonus, longing for oblivion.]

Epeius

The man who made the Wooden Horse by means of which the Greeks managed to enter Troy.

Epigoni

The sons of the Seven Against Thebes. Of the original Seven only one, Adrastus, escaped with his life. Ten years later he led the Epigoni in a second attack on Thebes and this time the city fell. Adrastus' own son, Aegialeus, was killed and Adrastus died of grief.

EPIMETHEUS

Epimetheus

See PANDORA.

Epona

The Roman goddess of horses and mules.

Erato

Muse of erotic poetry.

Erebus

The mysterious darkness under the earth (sprung from Chaos) through which the dead had to pass to reach the realm of Pluto. CHARON was the son of Erebus.

Erechtheus

A legendary king of Athens who sacrificed one of his three daughters to save his country. The other two killed themselves. He is sometimes identified with ERICHTHONIUS.

Erichthonius

The son of the semen of Hephaestus as he struggled to overpower Athena. She reared the child but kept him in a chest guarded by serpents. She had given the chest into the keeping of the daughters of Cecrops with orders not to open it. But they opened it and terrified by what they saw (the child was part serpent) leaped from the Acropolis and killed themselves. Erichthonius became king of Athens. He invented the chariot and among his possessions were two drops of the Gorgon's blood, given to him by Athena.

Erigone

Daughter of ICARIUS. When her father was killed she was led to his body by their faithful dog Maera and, overcome with grief, killed herself. All three were placed among the stars. Icarius became the constellation Boötes, Erigone became Virgo, and Maera became Canicula.

Erinyes

See EUMENIDES.

Eriphyle

Amphiaraus married Eriphyle, sister of King ADRASTUS. Being a seer, Amphiaraus knew that the expedition against Thebes was doomed to failure but had agreed to abide by his wife's decision on whether or not he should accompany it. Polynices bribed her with the fatal necklace of HARMONIA to urge her husband to go. Amphiaraus went but cursed her and commanded his son to avenge his death. Whether Amphiaraus died or not is a matter of definition: a thunderbolt opened a hole in the earth and he disappeared into the hole and was never seen more—though he continued to exist as a spirit of prophecy. His son Alcmaeon, however, accepted it as death and later slew his mother to avenge his father.

Eris

Goddess of discord, daughter of Night, sister of Ares, and the mother of strife, in various forms and under various names.

The best-known incident connected with her is her coming (uninvited) to the wedding of Peleus and Thetis and throwing upon the table the fatal apple inscribed "For the fairest," an act which led to a quarrel among the greatest of the goddesses, gave Helen to Paris (for awarding the apple to Aphrodite), and so precipitated the Trojan War.

Eros

The god of love. In early Greek mythology he is the child of Chaos, antedating the Olympian gods. In later legends he is the son of Aphrodite—by various fathers: Zeus, Ares, or Hermes—and is represented as a winged boy. The older view sees him as a great creative, cohesive force in men's lives—the builder of cities, the establisher of friendships, etc. The later saw him more exclusively as the god of sensual desire and, as such, cruel and imperious. The Romans saw him almost entirely in this role, a winged child with a bow from which he shot the arrows of desire. Their name for him was *Cupid* and their concept has almost entirely replaced the older one in the modern mind.

Erymanthian Boar

Hercules' fourth labor was the capture of a wild boar that lived on Mount Erymanthus and ravaged the borders of Arcadia and Achaea. The task was assigned to Hercules in midwinter, which should have made it harder; but he made use of the weather, driving the boar (by shouting) out from its cover into the snow, where it floundered. He bound it with chains and dragged it to Eurystheus.

Erymanthus

1. A mountain on which lived the Erymanthian Boar, a ferocious beast whose capture constituted Hercules' fourth labor.
2. Son of Apollo, blinded by Aphrodite because he had seen her bathing. Apollo, in retaliation, assumed the form of a boar and killed Aphrodite's lover ADONIS.

Erysichthon

A Thessalian who cut down a grove of trees sacred to Demeter, despite the goddess' protest. In punishment he was afflicted with an insatiable and ruinous appetite. Indeed, a fatal appetite: ultimately his insatiable hunger led him to eat his own legs, thereby causing his death.

There is another story about him—unusually whimsical for mythology—that says that his daughter, in return for amorous favors granted Poseidon, was given the power to assume the shapes of various animals. She would assume one shape and her father would sell her. Then she would secretly resume her proper shape and come home to be sold again.

Erytheia

One of the HESPERIDES.

Eteocles

King of Thebes, son of Oedipus and Jocasta and brother of Polynices. To ensure peace the brothers agreed to rule the city on alternate years. But when the time came to relinquish his power to his brother, Eteocles refused. This led to the expedition of the Seven Against Thebes. The brothers met in battle and killed each other.

Eubuleus

The swineherd who told Demeter of the rape of her daughter Persephone.

Eumaeus

A swineherd who, after twenty years, remained faithful to his absent master, Odysseus, and fought by his side against the suitors.

EUMENIDES

Eumenides

[Eumenides is a euphemism, meaning "the kindly ones." They are also called the *Erinyes,* "the angry ones." Or they are called the *Furies,* from the violence of their pursuit and punishment of offenders.]

Springing from Gaea, as the blood of the mutilated Uranus fell upon the earth, they antedate the Olympian gods. Their function is to avenge violations of the natural order, including among such violations gross inhumanity. Heraclitus *(c.* 500 B.C.) said that if the sun deviated from his course the Eumenides would put him back on his proper track. They prohibited Hera from endowing the horse Xanthus with speech, because such an ability is unnatural in a horse. They are pitiless. They make no allowance for circumstances; only the deed concerns them. They pursue Orestes because, despite the fact that he acted in compliance with a direct command from one of the greatest of the gods, he committed matricide.

There are three of them: Alecto (the unresting), Megaera (the jealous), and Tisiphone (the avenger). They were represented as hideous old women with bloodshot eyes and with snakes for hair. They punished by arousing frenzies of remorse. The very sight of them drove the guilty mad with fear.

See IBYCUS, THE CRANES OF.

Eunomia

One of the HORAE.

Eupeithes

The father of the most insolent suitor in the *Odyssey.* After his son's death he leads an angry crowd of other grief-stricken fathers out to Laertes' farm to kill Odysseus. Odys-

seus kills Eupeithes with the first throw of his spear and
Athena, in the guise of Mentor, persuades those who remain
to accept what has happened and to provoke no more blood-
shed.

Euphorbus

A Trojan warrior who, seeing Patroclus helpless after Apollo
(concealed in a mist) had struck him severely from behind,
wounded him. However, he was himself almost immediately
killed by Menelaus.

[A modern, respectable Christian is always startled at the
immorality, by our standards, of the Greek gods. A good
prescription for lessening this amazement is a careful
perusual of the Old Testament.]

Euphrosyne

One of the GRACES.

[Milton, in *L'Allegro,* states two accounts of her parentage:

> But come, thou Goddess fair and free,
> In heaven yclep'd Euphrosyne,
> And by men, heart-easing Mirth,
> Whom lovely Venus at a birth
> With two sister Graces more
> To ivy-crowned Bacchus bore;
> Or whether (as some sager sing)
> The frolic wind that breathes the spring,
> Zephyr with Aurora playing,
> As he met her once a-Maying,
> There on beds of violets blue,
> And fresh-blown roses washed in dew,
> Filled her with thee, a daughter fair,
> So buxom, blithe, and debonair.]

EUROPA

Europa

Daughter of Agenor, sister of Cadmus and mother (by Zeus) of MINOS and RHADAMANTHUS and, according to later accounts, of SARPEDON. Zeus gave her the first robot, the bronze man TALUS, and various other magic gifts. Though in some versions it was Hephaestus who gave her Talus. But the best-known thing in her legend is that Zeus wooed her and bore her across the sea to Crete in the form of a white bull.

Eurus

God of the East Wind, brother of Boreas (the North Wind), Zephyrus (the West Wind), and Notus (the South Wind).

Euryalus

A young Phaeacian, in the *Odyssey,* who taunts the as-yet-unidentified Odysseus and thus gives him a proper opportunity of displaying his great skill and heroic strength.

Eurycleia

Odysseus' old nurse. As she washes his feet, she recognizes him by a scar on his leg, the result of a wound he had received as a young man in a boar hunt.

Eurydice

1. The wife of ORPHEUS. She died as the result of a snakebite and her husband, grief-stricken, went down into the underworld and by his music "Drew iron tears down Pluto's cheek/ And made Hell grant what love did seek"—namely, her release to return to the upper world. Hades (Pluto) granted the request on condition that she must follow Orpheus and that he must not look back until they had com-

pletely regained the upper world. But Orpheus couldn't resist looking back and so lost her.

2. Wife of Creon, king of Thebes, and mother of Haemon *(see* ANTIGONE).

Eurylochus

One of Odysseus' officers. When his men fell into Circe's hands and were turned into swine, he alone—suspecting magic and therefore cautiously lurking at a distance—managed to escape and carry the news to Odysseus. He later led Odysseus' men in their slaughter of the Oxen of the Sun—for which he, with all the men, were destroyed when Zeus struck the ship with a thunderbolt.

Eurymachus

One of the most insolent of the suitors in the *Odyssey*. He is spokesman for the others in demanding that Penelope select one of them as her husband. He throws a stool at the disguised Odysseus—and is the second suitor to be killed.

Eurynome

1. In one account of the Creation, Eurynome was the goddess of All. She rose naked from Chaos and, finding nothing to stand on, divided the sea from the sky. The movements of her body created a wind by which she became pregnant and produced Ophion, the great serpent. She then laid an egg which, at her bidding, Ophion hatched and out of it fell all things. Eurynome and Ophion lived on Mount Olympus—until she banished him to the underworld (for boasting that *he* had started the universe). She then created the Titans and was in time deposed by Saturn.

[Milton, in *Paradise Lost* (X, 580 ff.) says that the fallen angels, having become serpents, claimed that a serpent—one of them—had first ruled Creation.]

2. In the *Iliad* we are told that Eurynome was the daughter of Oceanus and Tethys and the mother, by Zeus, of the Graces.

Eurypylus

A warrior who fought against the Greeks at Troy. Pausanias (second century A.D.) relates that a chest came into Eurypylus' possession that had formerly belonged to Aeneas or Cassandra. It contained an image of Dionysus, the work of Hephaestus, and at the sight of it Eurypylus went mad.

Eurystheus

Cousin of HERCULES, to obey whose commands Hercules was bound in expiation of the murder (in a fit of insanity) of his own wife and children. The tasks which Eurystheus laid upon Hercules are known as the *Twelve Labors of Hercules*. After Hercules' death Eurystheus was killed by Hyllus, Hercules' son (or by Iolaus, his nephew).

Euryton

A giant who, with a two-headed dog, guarded the oxen of the monster Geryon. He was killed by Hercules in the course of his tenth labor—which required him to capture these oxen.

Euterpe

Muse of the flute and Dionysiac music.

Evadne

The wife of Capaneus, one of the Seven Against Thebes. When he was killed she burned herself on his pyre.

Evander

The Arcadian chief who had preceded Aeneas to Italy many years before the fall of Troy. He was an enemy of Turnus and the Rutulians and became an ally of Aeneas and gained him the assistance of the Etruscans.

Evelake

Sir Evelake (or *Mordrayns)*, a wounded knight, in Malory's *Morte d'Arthur* who, nonetheless, is four hundred years old. He owes his longevity to having asked God to let him live until he sees the knight who will find the Holy Grail.

Evocatio

Every city in antiquity was protected by one or more tutelary deities. If the city were taken, the gods might become the possession, as it were, of the conquerors. But more commonly if the gods foresaw ruin for the city, they would fly from it, and their going greatly increased the chances—or, rather, marked the certainty—of its fall. Thus Plutarch tells us that the night before Alexandria fell to Octavius Caesar, the god Hercules left the city and deserted Antony.

There was a regular military procedure in a siege called the *Evocatio*—the "calling out" or "summoning" of the resident gods to leave the city. They were usually offered greater honors and fuller rites in the city of the besieger if they would heed the call.

Excalibur

King Arthur's sword, which, when he was but a boy, he drew out of a stone from which no one else could pull it. This account is in Malory's *Morte d'Arthur,* where it is also said that it was given to him by the Lady of the Lake. When

EXCALIBUR

Arthur was dying he commanded Sir Bedivere to throw Excalibur into the water and as it fell a hand rose from the water, seized and brandished the sword, and then disappeared with the sword beneath the surface.

In the older version by Geoffrey of Monmouth, the sword is called *Caliburn*.

Fafnir (Norse), **Fafner** (in Wagner's *Ring*)

In the *Volsung Saga* Fafnir is a dragon guarding Andvari's gold hoard. Sigurd, riding Greyfell, slew Fafnir on Glistenheath and, eating his heart, learned the speech of birds.

In Wagner's *Ring*, Fafner and his brother Fasolt are giants who built Valhalla for Wotan on condition that they be given the goddess Freya as payment. Fasolt accepts Alberich's gold in place of the goddess and Fafner kills Fasolt and changes himself into a dragon to guard the hoard.

Fate

In the sense of a predetermined, suprahuman, overriding Necessity, fate, in the Greek legends, is usually the equivalent of destiny, or "the will of Zeus." But as there were forces older than the gods and some, such as the Eumenides, that refused to acknowledge the supreme power of the Olympians, the word—though rarely, and then only vaguely—suggests some Necessity before which even the gods must bow. Thus Zeus has to send *two* doves to bring his ambrosia, since one is always crushed by the Crashing Rocks. It's a trifle, a mere celestial inconvenience, but it suggests that there is something that limits even the greatest power. In the *Iliad* some of the gods wish to save Hector. But Zeus weighs the

FATES

scales and states that it is "fated" that Hector die and he tells
the other gods that it will be useless for them to intervene.

In Norse mythology this is carried much further: the Frost
Giants are dangerous enemies who hold the gods, in Asgärd,
in a state of siege and will, at Ragnarok, destroy them.

Fates

The Fates, as distinct from the vaguer Fate, were the con-
trollers of individual human destinies, carrying out the will of
the gods. Called in Greek *Moerae* and in Latin *Parcae,* they
were conceived of as old women who were present at every
birth. They are Lachesis, who assigns the individual his lot
or fate; Clotho, who spins the thread of life; and Atropos
(= "the one who cannot be restrained"), who with "th' ab-
horred shears" cuts the thread of life.

See also NORNS.

Faunus

The Roman god of herdsmen and forests and bucolic revelry
and merrymaking. He came to be identified with the Greek
Pan, with whom he shared the power of being able to inspire
men with overpowering terror (cf. *panic).*

Fenrir (or **Fenris-wolf**)

The wolf monster, in Norse mythology, that is conceived by
Loki, is stronger than all the gods, and at Ragnarok will swallow the sun and kill Odin. But after Odin's death he will be
torn in two by Vidar, Odin's giant son.

One of the most famous stories connected with Fenrir concerns the forging of the cord that bound him. The gods asked
the dwarfs to make such a cord and they fashioned it from
the noise of a cat's footfall, the beards of women, the roots of
stones, the breath of fish, and the spit of birds. When the

gods asked the monster to consent to be bound with this flimsy filament, they pretended it was all a joke, a ludicrous test of the monster's strength. But the wolf knew the gods all too well to trust them and would consent to be bound only on condition that Tyr place his hand in Fenrir's mouth—and bit the hand off when he found that the cord was magic and could not be broken. At Ragnarok, however, he will be free to do his evil deeds.

Finn

The father of Ossian, in Celtic mythology. As a child he touched the magic salmon of knowledge and, sucking his thumb, became possessed of all knowledge.

Flora

The Roman goddess of flowering plants and fertility in general. Her rites were celebrated in the last days of April and marked by spectacularly indecent mimings and farces.

Fortuna

The Roman goddess of good luck, analogue of the Greek TYCHE. She was especially the bringer of good luck to young married women in the form of fertility and a happy delivery.

[Of all the Roman gods or goddesses she was the one most spoken of in the Middle Ages and the Renaissance. She was pictured with a wheel—whose turning was a symbol of the ceaseless rise and fall of felicity and misery.]

Frey (or Freyr)

The Norse god of weather and fruitfulness and hence the protector of marriage. His wife was Gerda. He was the patron of seafarers and owned the ship SKIDBLADNIR and the boar with golden bristles, Gullinbursti—on which he could ride through the air with incredible speed.

Freya

In Norse mythology, the daughter of Njord, the sister of Frey, the wife of Odin, and the mother of Noss, a daughter. She is the goddess of love, beauty, and fertility, the Norse equivalent of Aphrodite. Friday is named in her honor.

[She is a very old goddess and it is thought that she became assimilated with Frigga. The d'Aulaires state that she was married to Od, who vanished and is thought by some to have changed into Odin.]

Frigga

The wife of Odin in Norse mythology, and queen of the gods. She was the mother of Balder, Hermod, Hoder, and—in some accounts—of Tyr. She is the goddess of married love and easily confused with Freya, also a wife of Odin.

Fulla, Gna, Lin

Frigga's ladies in waiting.

Furies

See EUMENIDES.

Gaea (also **Gaia, Ge**)

The earth goddess whose name is the first syllable of *geography, geometry, geology,* etc. The offspring of Chaos, she of herself begot Uranus (heaven) and Pontus (ocean). By Uranus she was the mother of the Cyclops, the Hecatoncheires ("the hundred-handed ones"), and the Titans. By Pontus she produced various sea creatures. The Erinyes sprang from her when the blood of the mutilated Uranus fell on her. She was, ultimately, the source of all life; hence the ancient custom of placing a newborn child upon the earth.

The Romans identified her with *Tellus.*

Gaheris

A knight of King Arthur's Round Table, son of King Lot and nephew of King Arthur. He had three brothers: GAWAIN, AGRAVAIN, and GARETH. He was accidentally killed by Sir Launcelot.

Galahad

Son of Launcelot and Elaine. Purest in heart of the knights of the Round Table ["My strength is as the strength of ten,/ Because my heart is pure"—Tennyson, *Sir Galahad*], he is destined to find the Holy GRAIL.

[Perhaps because it has suggestive echo of *gallant,* his

name has become a term for exquisite courtesy as well as spotless purity.]

Galahalt (or **Galahault**)

The prince of the Long Isles who, in Malory's *Morte d'Arthur* introduces Launcelot to Queen Guinevere.

[There is a reference to him, under the name of Galeotto in Dante's *Inferno* (V, 137).]

Galatea

1. A sea nymph beloved by the youth Acis, son of Faunus. However, Polyphemus, the one-eyed Cyclops, loved her also and when she rejected his suit he crushed Acis under a huge rock. In one version she escaped by diving into the sea and later changed Acis into a river. In another she wept so copiously that she was changed into a fountain. In still a third version she accepted Polyphemus and had by him a son, Galates, ancestor of the Gauls.

2. The mother of a daughter, Leucippus, who was reared as a boy in order to deceive her husband, who had commanded the child to be killed at birth if it were a girl. Galatea's prayers to Leto were answered by changing the daughter's sex.

3. The name of the statue which Pygmalion made and fell in love with and which Aphrodite gave life to. The application of Galatea to this statue is, however, a modern, not an ancient application.

Galinthias (or **Galanthis**)

A servant of Alcmene's. When Alcmene was bearing Hercules, the Moerae (see FATES) prevented the birth by sitting with their knees held together and their hands clasped around their knees. Galinthias, learning of this, ran out shouting that Alcmene had given birth to a child. This so startled the Moerae (for it could not happen while they maintained their magical position—and hence its happening, if it *had* happened, meant the end of their power, the subversion of the whole order of things) started to their feet and in so doing freed Alcmene's thighs and her child was born. According to Ovid, the Moerae were so angered by this trick that they turned the subtle, darting Galinthias into a lizard.

Ganesa

The god of wisdom in Vedic mythology. He is usually represented with the head of an elephant.

Ganymede

A beautiful Trojan youth made immortal and taken up to Olympus to be cupbearer to the gods, supplanting in that office HEBE.

Gareth

Son of King Lot of Orkney. Hence brother to Gawain, Agravain, and Gaheris. He presented himself at King Arthur's court in disguise and served as a scullion under Sir Kay, the seneschal, who scornfully called him *Beaumains* (="pretty hands"). Lynet, a damsel, comes to the court seeking aid for her sister Lyonors, who is besieged in her castle by four knights. To her disgust the kitchen knave is assigned the quest—which he not only brings to a successful conclusion but wins her hand in marriage, or that of her rescued sister.

[Tennyson retold the story in "Gareth and Lynette" in *The Idylls of the King.*]

GARM

Garm

The Norse analogue of Cerberus—the snarling dog that guarded the gate of Hel. At Ragnarok he will kill and be killed by Tyr.

Gawain

In Malory's *Morte d'Arthur* Sir Gawain is the perfect knight. He is the son of Morgause, wife of King Lot of Orkney and sister of King Arthur. Gawain is the brother of Agravain, Gaheris, and Gareth, and is the enemy of Sir Launcelot. He is killed in the fighting at Dover when Arthur returns to suppress Modred's treacherous rebellion.

His most famous adventure (not in Mallory but in a long, alliterative fourteenth-century poem) was his encounter with Bercilak de Hautdesert, the "Green Knight." All of the knights are challenged by the strange giant to a beheading contest, the knight to be allowed the first stroke. Gawain beheaded the Green Knight, who calmly picked up his head and commanded Gawain to meet him at a lonely chapel a year from that time to receive the counterstroke. Gawain kept the tryst, after several temptations which he resists almost, but not quite, perfectly. The Green Knight spared his life but wounded him slightly.

[That Gawain's strength increases until noon and declines thereafter suggests that he may originally have been a sun god.]

Geirrod

A powerful Jotun who seized Loki and would not release him until he had promised to bring Thor, unarmed, to Geirrod's hall. Loki, by lying, inveigled Thor into going, but the giantess Grid warned Thor of the danger and gave him a magic mitten, a magic belt, and a magic staff. There was an ex-change of Jotunesque lethal horseplay in the course of which Thor, because of possessing the mitten, belt, and staff, was able to kill the giant.

[There is a curious incident in this story. As Thor and Loki, on their way to Geirrod's hall, were fording a stream, the volume of water suddenly increased with impetuous violence and but for the magic staff they would have been drowned. The spate, or freshet, it turned out, was caused by one of Geirrod's daughters, who was urinating upstream, with malice and micturition aforethought. The incident is so charmingly Norse and so utterly *un*Greek.]

Genius

See DAEMON.

Geryon

A winged, three-headed, three-bodied monster who lived on the island of Erytheia and had a herd of man-eating cattle which was guarded by a two-headed dog, Orthros, and a fierce shepherd. To bring back these cattle was the tenth labor of Hercules—which he accomplished, though he had to kill Geryon, the shepherd, and the dog.

Gialler Horn (or **Gjaller Horn**)

The warning horn of HEIMDAL, the guardian of the Rainbow Bridge in Norse mythology. If sounded softly, it announced the passage over the bridge of one of the gods. If loudly, it warned of the approach of a giant. The blast that announces Ragnarok will shake the world.

GIANTS

Giants

Offspring of Gaea and Uranus, the giants were sometimes represented as huge warriors and sometimes as monsters with snakes for legs. In mythology they engage in a ferocious war with the gods, by whom (assisted by Hercules) they are destroyed. As in most heroic accounts of battle, the struggle is an endless series of personal combats. Thus Zeus destroys Porphyrion with a thunderbolt. Poseidon crushes Polybotes by throwing an island on him. Hercules kills Alcyoneus, Antaeus, and others. Even Dionysus joins in, entangling several giants in his vine.

Gimlé

The new heaven that will replace (or has replaced) Asgärd after Ragnarok when there will be (or is) only a single God, the great God Almighty.

[The alternative verbs are necessitated by one's religion. Since we know of no cataclysm anything like Ragnarok having occurred since the time of the *Eddas* (ninth and thirteenth centuries, A.D.), we must assume that Ragnarok has not yet taken place and the Aesir still reign. Christians, however, who accept the one, all-powerful God, must assume that the old gods have disappeared, and Ragnarok was the only way they *could* disappear. Some scholars believe the Gimlé and the single God was an addition by the Christian missionaries bringing the go(d)-spel.]

Ginnungagap

The primeval abyss, in Norse mythology, whence—out of the mist created by the meeting of heat and cold—come all living things.

Gladsheim

The abode of the gods in Norse mythology. Vingolf was the abode of the goddesses. The most beautiful of all the palaces at Gladsheim was Valhalla, Odin's great hall.

Glauce (also called **Creusa**)

Daughter of Creon, king of Corinth. JASON deserted MEDEA for Glauce. Medea, in retaliation, killed Glauce and her father, and her own children by Jason.

[Considering that Medea had already shown that she possessed supernatural powers and almost supernatural ruthlessness and a firm determination to have her own way—having murdered and dismembered her own little brother to facilitate her elopement with Jason and, later, having fiendishly arranged for the daughters of PELIAS to kill their father unwittingly—considering all this, Jason must be regarded as a stupid hero or a hero of stupidity.]

Glaucus

1. Son of Hippolochus of Lycia, an ally of the Trojans in the Trojan War. He encountered Diomedes on the field of battle and discovering that they were hereditary guest-friends exchanged armor with him. The armor of Glaucus, however, was gold and that of Diomedes was bronze and the exchange became proverbial for getting the worst of a bargain. Glaucus was later killed by Ajax.

2. Son of Minos and Pasiphaë. He was drowned in a vat of honey but was revived by the soothsayer Polyeidus.

3. Steersman of the ship *Argo*. He loved Scylla—before she was changed into a monster. Circe loved him. He became a sea divinity.

4. A charioteer, son of Sisyphus and father of Bellerophon.

GLEIPNIR

He fed his horses human flesh and, growing accustomed to the diet, they finally devoured him. After death he became a Taraxippos—that is, "horse-scarer," a spook that specialized in scaring race horses at highly critical moments in races.

Gleipnir

The magic skein which the dwarfs, in Norse mythology, wove to bind the wolf Fenrir. It was made of the sound of a cat's footsteps, the roots of stones, the beards of women, and the spittle of birds. It seemed fragile but was unbreakable. The gods persuaded Fenrir to allow himself to be bound with it, as a joke. But, just to be on the safe side, he insisted that Tyr, the warrior god, place his hand in his mouth, and when Fenrir found that the thread was magic, he bit Tyr's hand off.

Golden Age

It was under the rule of Cronus (or Saturn, to the Romans), before the rule of Zeus, that the Golden Age had existed. It was a time of peace and abundance, a time when the earth produced plentifully without being tilled and men in happy idleness and glowing health lived to a great age.

[All times have dreamed of a Golden Age. We differ from previous ages in placing our Golden Age in the future. A modern is a little puzzled at the indiscretion, to call it nothing worse, of the ancients placing their Golden Age *before* the reign of Zeus.]

Golden Bough

In the grove of Nemi or Aricia near Rome, sacred to the goddess Diana, there ruled a priest—usually a runaway slave —who gained his office by first plucking a bough from a certain tree in the grove and then killing, in single combat, the priest-king already in possession. The killer then became ruler of the grove and remained such until he was killed by his successor:

> Those trees in whose grim shadow
> The ghastly priest doth reign,
> The priest who slew the slayer,
> And shall himself be slain.
> —Macaulay, *Battle of Lake Regillus,* X

Aeneas (Book VI of the *Aeneid)*, at the instruction of the Cumaean Sybil, plucked a golden bough from a tree in this grove and by showing the bough persuaded the reluctant Charon to ferry him, living as he was, over the Styx to the underworld.

Diana was worshipped in the grove as a wood goddess, in conjunction with an obscure male deity Virbius. The mystery —even for mythology—of these peculiar circumstances was the stimulus that led Sir James Frazer to do his famous twelve-volume work on folklore, mythology, and religion, *The Golden Bough,* that did much to establish the science of anthropology.

Golden Fleece

Athamas, son of Aeolus, had two children by his first wife, Nephele: a son, Phrixus, and a daughter, Helle. Nephele died. Athamas then married Ino, a daughter of Cadmus, by whom he had two sons, Learchus and Melicertes. Ino hated the children of her husband's first marriage and to save them from her hatred the shade of Nephele brought them a ram with a Golden Fleece on whose back (since it could fly) they could escape. As the magic ram was crossing the strait between Europe and Asia, however, Helle fell from its back—

and the strait was thereafter called the *Hellespont.* Phrixus, however, reached the farther shore and went on to Colchis, where he sacrificed the ram to Zeus and hung up its Golden Fleece in the temple of Ares. Later it was hung on a tree in a sacred grove and guarded by an unsleeping dragon.

The fetching of the fleece from Colchis was the task which King Pelias lay on the hero Jason.

See ARGONAUTS, MEDEA.

Gordian Knot

Gordius, the father of Midas, was made king of Phrygia when his entry into a city happened to correspond with an oracular prediction. He tied his wagon in the temple with a knot of extreme intricacy which, it was said, no one but the destined ruler of all Asia could undo. Alexander the Great—impatient, contemptuous, inspired, or well advised by a good public relations man—cut the knot with his sword.

Gorgons

Three frightful sisters, daughters of Phorcys and Ceto. They had snakes for hair and to look on them turned men to stone. Their names were Stheno ("the mighty"), Euryale ("the wide-wandering"), and Medusa ("the cunning one"), sometimes called Medusa the Queen. She, the youngest of the three, alone among them was mortal, and was eventually slain by PERSEUS, who killed her—with the aid of various magic accouterments—by looking in a mirror and striking backwards with his sword. At the moment of her death she was pregnant by Poseidon and from her blood sprang Pegasus, the winged horse, and Chrysaor, the monster who later fathered Geryon and Echidna.

Medusa's petrifying head adorned the aegis of Zeus and Athena.

[In early representations the Gorgons were represented as something like childish Hallowe'en false faces, with protruding eyes and huge serrated teeth. But under the influence of more poetic inspiration they, especially Medusa, came to be pictured as beautiful, with the snaky locks stylized to little more than a comedy wave. Shelley *(On the Medusa)* aptly perceived that "it is less the horror than the grace/ Which turns the gazer's spirit into stone." Milton *(Comus)* felt that it was "rigid looks of chaste austerity" in a virgin that froze (presumptuous males, no doubt) "to congeal stone."]

Graces (also called Charites)

In some accounts daughters of Zeus and EURYNOME; in others, daughters of Aphrodite and Dionysus. There are three of them: Euphrosyne, Aglaia, and Thalia. They attend upon Hera and Aphrodite—though Athena sometimes calls them in to aid her, because without grace all labor is vain. Hermes uses them, too, since he is the god of oratory.

Their concern is with decorum, purity, happiness, goodwill, kindness, and gratitude. They preside over banquets and social activities in general.

Graiae

Daughters of Phorcys and Ceto, sisters of the Gorgons, there are three of them: Pemphredo, Dino, and Enyo. Represented as three aged women—they were born gray-haired—with only one eye and one tooth among them, they alone knew where the Gorgons were to be found and protected them by being on the lookout for approaching danger. But Perseus stole their eye (as they passed it from one to another) and would not restore it until they had told him where to find Medusa.

GRAIL

Grail

Commonly known as the Holy Grail, this was the cup from which Christ drank at the Last Supper and which later, at the Crucifixion, received the blood which flowed from the spear thrust in his side. It was brought to England by Joseph of Arimathea and, somehow, was lost. According to other accounts, it was brought by angels and guarded on top of a mountain. If anyone in any way impure approached it, it became invisible. The search for the Grail occupies Books XIII–XVIII of Malory's *Morte d'Arthur*. Sir Galahad is the pure knight who finally succeeds in the quest.

See ROUND TABLE, GALAHAD.

Gram

Sigurd's sword, in Norse mythology. It was forged for him by the smith Regin out of the fragments of his father Sigmund's sword.

Greyfell

Sigurd's horse, of the blood of Odin's horse Sleipnir.

Grid

A giantess, wife of Odin. At Ragnarok her son (by Odin), Vidar, will slay the Fenris-wolf.

Grimhild

In Norse mythology, the mother of Gudrun. She gave SIGURD a magic potion which made him lose all memory of Brunhild, so that he loved and married Gudrun. At the wedding feast of Gunnar and Brunhild, Grimhild's potion no longer had effect and Sigurd knew that he loved Brunhild.

Gryphon (or **Griffin**)

An animal with the body of a lion and the head and wings of an eagle. It guarded gold and warred eternally with the Arimaspians, a Scythian people endowed with only one eye and an insatiable lust to steal gold.

[As an emblem of valor and magnanimity, the Griffin is much employed in heraldry, on coats of arms.]

Gudrun

The counterpart, in the *Volsung Saga,* of Kriemhild in the *Nibelungenlied.*

Guinevere (also **Guanhamara, Gvenour, Wenhaver**)

The wife of ARTHUR in Malory's *Morte d'Arthur* and elsewhere. She loved Sir Launcelot and was faithless to Arthur.
See ARTHUR, LAUNCELOT.

Gungir

Odin's spear, made by the dwarfs.

Gunnar

King of the Nibelungs. In a magic forgetfulness and disguise Sigurd wooed Brunhild for Gunnar. Refusing to reveal the whereabouts of the Nibelung treasure to Atli, Gunnar was thrown into a den of poisonous snakes and fatally bitten by the only one that had not been charmed by his harp-playing.

Gunther

A Burgundian king in the *Nibelungenlied.* He is the brother of Kriemhild, the wife of Siegfried. He desires to marry Brunhild but is afraid to ride through the flames that surround her castle—a feat which she requires of any man who would seek to marry her. Siegfried, in Gunther's likeness, rides through the flames and spends three nights with Brunhild but keeps a sword between them all of the time. She marries Gunther but later learns that it was not he, but Siegfried, who had ridden through the flames, and where there had been amity between the two married pairs there was jealousy and enmity. Siegfried is murdered, Gunther being privy to the assassination. He himself is killed by his sister Kriemhild, Siegfried's widow.

Gymir

A Jotun, father of the beautiful Gerd who became the wife of Frey.

Hades (in Roman mythology also called **Dis, Orcus,** or **Pluto**)

He is the son of Cronus, the brother of Zeus, and the husband of Persephone. At the division of the world after the overthrow of Cronus, Zeus took the sky and the earth, Poseidon the sea, and Hades the underworld. Hades is gloomy, stern, and deaf to all appeals, so no sacrifices were offered to him. Aside from the rape of Persephone *(see* DEMETER), there are practically no legends relating to him. He came to be mixed up with Plutus, the god of wealth, and the place of his abode came to be referred to by his name as Hades. But the Greek realm of the dead has no resemblance to the Christian hell. It was in no sense a place of punishment. But neither was it a place of pleasure. It was a place of dim and endless dullness.

For the five rivers of Hades, *see* ACHERON, COCYTUS, LETHE, PHLEGETHON, and STYX.

Haemon

Son of Creon, king of Thebes. He was in love with and engaged to ANTIGONE. He killed himself when his father sentenced Antigone to death.

HAGEN

Hagen

The murderer of Siegfried in the *Nibelungenlied* who was himself killed by Kriemhild. In the *Volsung Saga* his name is *Högni*.

Halcyone (or **Alcyone**)

Ceyx, king of Trachis, disregarding the entreaties of his wife Halcyone (who, as a daughter of Aeolus, knew the power of the sea winds), sailed to Ionia to consult the oracle of Apollo, and was shipwrecked and drowned. All naked and dripping, he appeared to her in a dream and told her of his death. She hastened to the seashore and his body (in accordance with his last prayer) was washed ashore at her feet. She leaped into the sea to kill herself, but the gods, taking pity, changed her and Ceyx into kingfishers and Zeus forbade the winds to blow for seven days prior to and seven days after the winter solstice when they are hatching their eggs in the nests on the sea.

> [There came the halcyon, whom the sea obeys,
> When she her nest upon the water lays.
> —Michael Drayton, "Noah's Flood"

> Amidst our arms as quiet you shall be
> As halcyon brooding on a winter's sea.
> —John Dryden

"Halcyon days" now, however, means not so much calm days as days of happiness and prosperity.]

Halirrhothius

A son of Poseidon. He violated ALCIPPE, for which he was killed by Ares, Alcippe's father. ARES was tried by the Areopagus.

Halitherses

The Ithacan soothsayer in the *Odyssey* who warns the suitors that Odysseus will return within the year. In the last book he attempts, with Medon, to persuade the grief-stricken and angered kinsmen of the slaughtered suitors to accept the dreadful fact of the bloody justice which has befallen the suitors and not to seek vengeance and, in so doing, perchance make things much worse for themselves.

Hamadryads

Nymphs as the inhabitant spirits of trees. A Hamadryad lived only so long as her particular tree lived.

> [Science . . .
> Who alterest all things with they peering eyes
> . . . .
> Hast thou not dragged Diana from her car?
> And driven the Hamadryad from the wood.
> —E. A. Poe, *Sonnet—To Science*]

Harmonia

Daughter of Ares and Aphrodite (or, in some accounts, of Zeus and Electra). She was married to Cadmus on the Acropolis of Thebes. For a wedding gift Cadmus gave her a necklace fashioned by Hephaestus. This with another gift, a jewelled robe, had the power of stirring up strife for whoever possessed it. They brought evil to all the descendants of Cadmus and to ERIPHYLE and to all the sons of Eriphyle. Eventually the fatal gifts were deposited in the shrine at Delphi.

Harpalyce

See ALASTOR.

Harpies

Three (in some accounts, two) winged creatures, daughters of Thaumas and Electra. They were sometimes represented as women with birds' wings, some times as birds with women's faces. They appear in the *Odyssey* as having snatched away the daughters of Pandareos "to serve the terrible Furies." They are best known for snatching away the food of Phineus, the blind seer, and so befouling what they did not bear away that he could not eat it. They were, however, driven off by CALAIS AND ZETES, sons of Boreas, who had arrived with the Argonauts, who needed certain advice from Phineus. The names of the Harpies, in various accounts, are: *Aello (pus), Ocypete, Celaeno, Podarge.*

[Phineus was a seer. He had been blinded by the Gods because he predicted the future *too* accurately! Plainly a soothsayer's life was not a happy one.]

Harpocrates

The Latin name for the Egyptian god Horus as a boy, represented as with a finger at his lips and so interpreted, by the Latins, as the god of discreet silence. A Roman legend stated that Cupid had bribed Harpocrates with a rose to keep secret certain amorous goings-on of Venus. Hence the rose as a symbol of silence. "Under the rose," in our common expression, seems to derive from the carving of a rose in the ceiling of medieval banqueting halls as a sign that the babblings of conviviality were privileged.

Hathor

The Egyptian goddess of beauty, love, and marriage. She attended at childbirth. As a sky goddess she wore the solar disk. As a mother goddess she was represented with a cow's head.

Hebe

The daughter of Zeus and Hera. She was the embodiment of youth and grace and was cupbearer to the gods until replaced by Ganymede.

Hecate

Granddaughter of Uranus and Rhea, Hecate—who had three bodies and three heads (those of a lion, a dog, and a mare)—was the only Titan to retain power after Zeus had overthrown her father Cronus. She is a mysterious, sinister goddess, connected variously with Demeter, Rhea, and Persephone. In her attendance upon Persephone, the goddess of the underworld, she became a spirit having to do with ghosts and witchcraft.

[Hecate is one of the "secret, black and midnight hags" to whom Macbeth goes after "the blood-boulter'd Banquo" had appeared at his solemn feast. Here she is "the close contriver of all harms" and dominant over the Weird Sisters. Lear, in his first explosion of rage, swears by "the mysteries of Hecate and the night"—though Kent's "Now by Apollo, King,/ Thou swear'st thy gods in vain" indicates that she was not regarded as a common fiend or deity.]

HECATONCHEIRES

Hecatoncheires

See BRIAREUS.

Hector

The oldest son of Priam, king of Troy, and of Hecuba, his queen. Hector is Troy's greatest warrior. He is the husband of Andromache, father of Astyanax, and brother of Paris (and forty-eight other brothers and half brothers). After various feats of arms with various Greek heroes, he kills Patroclus, the dear friend of Achilles (who was sulking in his tent because the maid Briseis had been taken from him by Agamemnon) and is himself killed by Achilles. His body was ignominiously dragged, behind Achilles' chariot, three times around the walls of Troy and then cast on a refuse heap. But his aged father ransomed his body and the *Iliad* ends with his funeral.

Hecuba

The second wife of Priam, king of Troy, to whom she bore nineteen of his fifty sons. She saw her sons and her husband killed, her infant grandson murdered, herself and her daughters enslaved. And so—and justly!—she stands as one of the supreme examples of suffering womanhood.

She was a figure of dignity and resolution, even in her misery. At the division of the spoils of Troy (in the post-Homeric legends) she was assigned to Odysseus. Touching the coast of Thrace on Odysseus' return, she learned that her last surviving son, Polydorus, who had been entrusted to King Polymestor, had been murdered by Polymestor. She and her women murdered Polymestor's children in his sight and then blinded him.

[Hecuba was the daughter, in one account, of Dymas of

Phrygia, in another of Cisseus. The identity of her mother was, apparently, a mystery even in antiquity. For Suetonius tells us that the Emperor Tiberius, who prided himself on his knowledge of mythology, used to taut the grammarians at his court by demanding to know what song the sirens sang, what name Achilles assumed when he hid among the maidens in Scyros, and "Who was Hecuba's mother?"]

Heidrun

Odin's goat, from whose udders was drawn a never-failing supply of mead for the Norse gods.

Heimdal

The watchman god in Norse mythology who keeps sleepless guard over the bridge Bifrost, awaiting the assault of the Frost Giants. He has his sword Höfud and his horn Gjallar, which he will sound when the attack begins. He can see as well by night as by day and can hear the wool growing on the backs of the sheep.

Hel (or Hela)

The Norse goddess of the underworld. She is the daughter of Loki and the giantess Angurboda. She is sister of the Fenriswolf and the Midgard Serpent. She dwelled in Niflheim and in her kingdom there were nine abodes or levels, descending from the level reserved for those who died of sickness or old age down to those who are consigned to some particular punishment. Her body has the lividness of death and her countenance is forbidding. Her hall is called *Eliudnir* (= "den of sleet"). She is waited on by Delay and Slowness.

HELEN

Helen

Daughter of Zeus and Leda (or of Zeus and Nemesis). She was the wife of Menelaus, king of Sparta, but was carried off by Paris, son of Priam, king of Troy. The suitors of Helen had agreed, in order to keep the peace, that whoever won her all would unite against anyone who attempted to interfere with the marriage. So her abduction led to the Trojan War. In Troy she was regarded as Paris' wife. After his death she married Deiphobus, another son of Priam's, whom she betrayed at the fall of the city. After the capture of Troy she returned to Sparta with Menelaus and was living there in quiet and dignified domesticity when visited by Telemachus, Odysseus' son, who was seeking news of his father.

After her death, it is said she married Achilles in the underworld.

Helenus

A seer, the son of Priam. He was captured by the Greeks and prophesied that Troy would fall if the Greeks enlisted the aid of PHILOCTETES.

Helicon

A mountain sacred to the Muses. Hippocrene, the fountain of poetic inspiration, had its source on Mount Helicon. It was opened by a kick of Pegasus' hoof.

Helios (Roman **Sol**)

The sun god, sometimes called *Hyperion,* though he was most commonly regarded as the son of the Titan Hyperion. He drove a chariot with four horses across the heavens every day, from east to west. Every night he floated back in a huge cup that was swept along in the current of the great ocean that surrounded the world. Because he saw everything, he was invoked to witness oaths.

Apollo is often confused with Helios in that he—Apollo—is the Olympian deity of the sun. But Helios is of an older generation than Apollo and represents the sun in its daily course, in its physical manifestation; whereas Apollo represents its brightness, its light, its healing power, etc.

Helle

See PHRIXUS AND HELLE.

Hellespont

See GOLDEN FLEECE.

Hemera

Personification of Day. She was the daughter of EREBUS and Night and the sister of Aether (Air).

Hephaestus (Roman Vulcan)

Son of Zeus and Hera, husband of Aphrodite, father of ERECHTHEUS. He was lame in consequence of having interfered in a quarrel between his parents; the enraged Zeus had thrown him over the battlements of heaven and he had been crippled when he landed (after falling a full day) on Lemnos. He was married to Aphrodite. She was false to him with Ares, and Hephaestus caught them in the act in a net which he had made and exposed them to the derision of the other gods.

Hephaestus was the god of the crafts, builder of palaces for the gods, forger of Zeus' thunderbolts. He made the armor of Achilles, the necklace of Harmonia, and the axe wherewith the skull of Zeus was split in order to facilitate the birth of Athena. And, above all, he made Pandora, the first woman. The Cyclops were his workmen and the volcanoes were the chimneys of his stithies. Still his identification by the Romans with Vulcan was inappropriate. For Hephaestus was primarily a fabricator and Vulcan was purely a god of destructive fire.

[Milton *(Paradise Lost,* I, 743) has a fine poetic description of Hephaestus' fall:

> . . . from morn
> To noon he fell, from noon to dewy eve,
> A summer's day, and with the setting sun
> Dropt from the zenith, like a falling star,
> On Lemnos, the Aegaean isle.]

Hera (identified by the Romans with their goddess **Juno**)

Daughter of Cronus and Rhea, she is Zeus' sister and his wife and second only to him among the Olympians. She is the mother of Ares, Hebe, and Hephaestus. She is the protectress of marriage, childbirth, and the home. Because Paris awarded the golden apple to Aphrodite (who stands for much of what Hera opposes), she is an enemy of the Trojans. She appears in a score of mythological stories as the jealous wife of philandering Zeus, harrying his mistresses and persecuting their children.

Hercules (Greek **Heracles**)

The greatest of the Greek heroes. He was the son of Zeus by Alcmene, wife of AMPHITRYON; hence he was sometimes called *Alcides,* after Alcaeus, father of Amphitryon. His whole life—from the very moment of his birth—was shaped by the animosity of Hera, who pursued him with relentless hostility. He was adopted by the Romans, who worshipped him as the god of physical strength.

Hera drove him mad and in his madness he killed his wife

and children. To expiate this crime (and to gain immortality) he served Eurystheus, king of Mycenae, for twelve years. And it was Eurystheus who set him the famous Twelve Labors which are one of the major features of his legend. They are (though different accounts assign a different order):

(1) The killing of the Nemean Lion
(2) The killing of the Hydra
(3) The capture of the Cerynean hind (or stag)
(4) The killing of the Erymanthian boar
(5) The cleansing of the Augean stables
(6) The killing of the birds of Stymphalus
(7) Capturing the Cretan bull
(8) Capturing the man-eating horses of Diomedes of Thrace
(9) Obtaining the girdle of Hippolyte, queen of the Amazons
(10) Capturing the oxen of Geryon
(11) Bringing back the Apples of the Hesperides
(12) Bringing up from Hades of Cerberus, the three-headed dog.

(The major labors are discussed under separate headings.)

Among other of his many legends may be mentioned his strangling of two serpents (sent by Hera) when he was but an infant in his cradle. One account says that they were not sent by Hera but were put in the way of the twins by Amphitryon in order to see which of them was his child and which Zeus'.

Other adventures included his rescuing of Hesione, daughter of Laomedon, king of Troy, who had promised him his famous horses as a reward. But once the rescue was effected, Laomedon refused to keep his word and Hercules sacked the city. He sailed with the Argonauts, but only part of the way; at Cios water nymphs carried off Hylas, Hercules' page, and Hercules took so long looking for him that the others, impatient, sailed away and left him—an act which he severely punished.

The details of Hercules' death by means of the poisoned blood of the Centaur Nessus may be found under DEIANIRA, LICHAS, and NESSUS. After his death he was taken up to Olympus, where he married Hebe.

In all Greek mythology Hercules was the most popular figure. He was essentially human—hot-tempered, gluttonous, and lustful, but—also human—he had pity for those in trouble and put his supernatural strength frequently at the disposal of the unfortunate. His deeds often include a large element of shrewdness—as in his holding Antaeus *off* the ground, in diverting the rivers through the Augean stables, in tricking Atlas into resuming the burden of the sky, etc.—and it may have been this that led to his becoming a comic figure on the Attic and the Roman stage. He was, in a way, the predecessor of Superman.

Hermaphroditus

Son of Hermes and Aphrodite, he was beloved by Salmacis, the nymph of a fountain. When he scorned her love, she prayed to be forever united with him and her prayer was answered: lover and beloved were combined in a single bisexual person.

Hermes (Roman **Mercury**)

Son of Zeus and MAIA. He was precocious. By noon of the day he was born he had left his cradle and invented the lyre, constructing it from the shell of a tortoise. The same day he drove off fifty cows belonging to his half brother Apollo (son of Zeus and Leto), making them walk backwards so that they could not be traced. Apollo traced them, however, and came on Hermes in a rage, but his anger was turned to delight when Hermes presented him with the lyre. He let Hermes keep the cattle, gave him various other gifts and, generally, made him his favorite.

Hermes was the god of good luck and wealth, the patron of merchants and thieves. [The Greeks in their primitive innocence saw a relationship here!] As the god of commerce he was the patron of deception—a skill with which he endowed his son Autolycus, "who surpassed all men in stealing and lying." Hermes was the god of roads and a god of fertility, functions that were both designated in the Hermae, quadrangular pillars with a bust of the god set on them and a phallus sculpted below.

Hermes was the messenger and herald of the gods and the conductor of the souls of the dead to Hades. He was also a god of sleep and dreams. He was represented as a young man with a broad-brimmed hat and winged sandals, and bearing the caduceus.

Hermione

Daughter of Menelaus and Helen. Wife of Neoptolemus and later of Orestes, to whom she bore a son, Tisamenus.

Hermod

Messenger of the Norse gods and official greeter (with his brother Bragi) of the heroes whom the Valkyries brought to Valhalla. His descent into Niflheim to persuade Hel to release Balder was futile.

HERO AND LEANDER

Hero and Leander

Hero was a priestess of Aphrodite at Sestos, a town on the European side of the Hellespont (what we now call the Dardanelles), at its narrowest point—which is about three-quarters of a mile wide, with a swift current. Leander, her lover, lived in Abydos, on the Asian side directly opposite, and swam across every night to see her, guided by a light which she kept burning. One night a storm extinguished the light and he was drowned. She then drowned herself.

[The story is the subject of poems by Christopher Marlowe and Thomas Hood. It was burlesqued by Thomas Nashe in his "Prayse of Red Herring."

Byron, feeling apparently that he must emulate other great lovers, swam the Hellespont in company with a Mr. Ekenhead, a performance with which, because of its poetic associations, he was rather pleased. His hero Don Juan, he says (II, cv), was an excellent swimmer:

> He could, perhaps, have pass'd the Hellespont, As once (a feat on which ourselves we prided) Leander, Mr. Ekenhead, and I did.]

Hesione

Poseidon and Apollo had assisted Laomedon in building the walls of Troy. But when the task was done Laomedon refused to pay them the wages he had agreed to pay. Poseidon sent a sea monster to ravage the country and Laomedon offered his daughter Hesione to the monster as a propitiation. Hercules appeared in the nick of time, however, and killed the monster. Poseidon remained angry and was opposed to the Trojans at the beginning of the Trojan War.

Hesperia

1. One of the Hesperides.
2. The name in ancient Greece for Italy and in ancient Italy for Spain.

Hesperides (= "children of the evening star," "children of the west")

Three sisters (some accounts say seven), daughters of Hesperus, the evening star, or of Atlas, who guarded the golden apples of Hera, with the assistance of the dragon Ladon. Some accounts state that the nymphs were eating the apples and Ladon was put there to guard the tree against its guardians. Hercules, as one of his Twelve Labors, slew the dragon and, with the help of the Titan Atlas carried off the apples.

> [Hesperus and his daughters three
> That sing about the golden tree.
> —John Milton]

Hestia (Roman **Vesta**)

Child of Cronus and Rhea, she is the goddess of the hearth, of peace, and the family. She is a virgin and of all the Olympians the most peaceful and mild.

Himeros

See ANTEROS.

Hippocampus

The horse upon which Neptune is frequently depicted as riding. It has the forelegs of a horse but its posterior end is that of a fish or dragon.

HIPPOCRENE

Hippocrene

See HELICON.

Hippogriff

A winged horse, offspring of a griffin and a filly. It had the head, wings, and claws of a griffin, and the body, hooves, and tail of a horse.

Hippolyte

Queen of the Amazons; daughter of Ares and Otrera. The securing of her girdle was Hercules' ninth labor. According to one account she was so impressed by his masculinity that she gave him the girdle, bringing it herself to his ship. Such uncharacteristic feminine amiability, however, led her women warriors to assume that she was being abducted and they attacked the ship. Whereupon Hercules, assuming the whole thing was an ambush, killed Hippolyte. Other accounts say that she survived to marry Theseus and bear him Hippolytus. Though still other accounts say that it was Antiope who bore this son.

See AMAZONS, HIPPOLYTUS.

Hippolytus

Son of Theseus by Hippolyte, queen of the Amazons, who was later killed by Hercules in pursuance of his labor of securing her girdle. Theseus then married Phaedra, daughter of Minos, who, during Theseus' absence made advances to Hippolytus, who rejected them. She then falsely accused Hippolytus of making advances to her. Theseus begged Poseidon to avenge him and the god sent a monster out of the sea which frightened Hippolytus' horses so that he was thrown from his chariot and dragged to his death. Phaedra hanged herself. Theseus learned the truth, but too late.

In some versions of the legend Hippolytus was restored to life by Aesculapius, an act which so offended Zeus that he destroyed Aesculapius with a thunderbolt.

Hoder (or Hodur, Hodr)

The blind son of Odin and Frey in Norse mythology. Tricked by Loki, Hoder killed his brother Balder by throwing a sprig of mistletoe at him. In some versions of the story Hoder is killed at Ragnarok; in others he survives and is, eventually, reconciled with his brother.

Hoenir

Brother of Odin, he was one of the three Aesir gods who made the world. Also called Vili. He was slow-witted and was sent by the Aesir to the Vanir as a hostage.

Horae

The goddesses in Greek mythology who presided over the seasons and the natural course of growing things. They controlled the weather, among other functions. In one account they are the daughters of Zeus and THEMIS. There were three of them: Eunomia (Order), Dice (Justice), and Eirene (Peace).

Horatius

Publius Horatius Cocles. A hero of Roman legend who, with Spurius Lartius and Titus Herminius, held back the entire Etruscan army, under Lars Porsena, at the narrow, wooden Sublician bridge until it could be destroyed and thus the way to Rome be blocked. In the commonest version, Horatius held his position until the bridge went down and then "with his armor on his back" swam the Tiber to safety. In another version he was drowned. Scholars think the story may be a confused remnant of something related to Hephaestus or the Cyclops.

Horus

An Egyptian sun god usually represented with a falcon's head. As the god of light he fights with Set, the god of darkness and evil. He appears as Horus the elder and Horus the son of Osiris. As the first of these, he has many names.

See also HARPOCRATES.

Hotei

The Japanese god of jollity and good luck. Represented (like our Santa Claus) as plump and merry, and like Santa a favorite with children.

Houri

The black-eyed damsels awaiting the pleasure of the faithful in the Islamic paradise. Every believer was to have seventy-two houris at his disposal.

[Tom Moore (perhaps a little wistfully) wrote:

> A Persian's heaven is easily made:
> 'Tis but black eyes and lemonade.

Most men would certainly prefer it to golden crowns and shouts of *Hallelujah!*]

Hreidmar

King of the dwarfs in the *Volsung Saga*. He was killed by his son Fafnir to gain a treasure which Hreidmar held.

Hrimfaxi

The horse of night, in Norse mythology, from whose bridle falls the dew.

Hugin and Munin

The two ravens—representing Thought and Memory—that, in Norse mythology, perched on Odin's shoulders. Every day they flew to earth and returned to Odin with the news.

Hvergelmir

A spring in Niflheim whence originated the twelve rivers that filled the abyss of Ginnungagap with ice. Home of the dragon Nidhug.

Hyacinthus

A youth beloved by Apollo. He was killed by being struck by a quoit which Apollo had thrown but which Zephyrus (the West Wind), who also loved the boy and was jealous, had deflected. From his blood the hyacinth sprang, its petals bearing markings which the Greeks interpreted as *Ai, Ai,* their word for woe.

> [Apollo with unweeting hand,
> Whilom did slay his dearly-loved mate,
> Young Hyacinth. . . .
> But then transformed him to a purple flower.
> —Milton, *On the Death of a Fair Infant*

> . . . that sanguine flower inscribed with woe.
> —Milton, *Lycidas*

HYADES

> Pitying the sad death
> Of Hyacinthus, when the cool breath
> Of Zephyr slew him.
> —Keats, *Endymion*]

Hyades

Nymphs, daughters of Atlas and Aethra; sisters of the Pleiads. They were the nurses of Dionysus. They were associated, as stars, with the rainy season. One story was that they cried themselves to death when their brother Hyas was killed.

> [. . . when
> Thro' scudding drifts the rainy Hyades
> Vext the dim sea.
> —Tennyson, *Ulysses*]

Hydra

A dragon with nine heads. As soon as one head was cut off two new ones grew in its place. Slaying this monster was one of Hercules' Twelve Labors. He solved the capital conundrum by searing each neck as he cut off the head. Sometimes called the Lernaean Hydra because it lived in Lake Lerna in Argolis.

Hygeia (or **Hygieia**)

The goddess of health, the daughter of Aesculapius.

Hylas

Son of Theiodamas, king of the Dryopes. Hercules ate one of Theiodamas' oxen. Theiodamas attacked Hercules and was killed. But Hercules made the king's son his page and was very fond of him and took him along when he went on the famous voyage with the Argonauts. On the island of Cios, however, Hylas, going to get water from a spring was pulled in by the nymphs, who were enamoured of him. Hercules spent so much time looking for Hylas that the Argonauts grew impatient and sailed away without him.

Hymen

The Greek god of marriage. Either the marriage song was named after him or he was a personification of the song. Usually said to be the son of Apollo and one of the Muses.

Various legends: that he lost his voice and life singing at the marriage of Dionysus and Ariadne; that he was an Athenian youth who, disguised as a girl, followed a maiden he loved to the festival of Demeter at Eleusis. He and some of the maidens were carried off by pirates. He slew the pirates and became the defender of all damsels.

Hyperboreans

A people who, living north of where the North Wind (Boreas) begins, enjoy perpetual warmth and sunshine. Their atmosphere, says Herodotus, consists of feathers.

[Some of the learned have attempted to explain the feathered atmosphere as snow. But the Greeks were familiar with snow. In Book XIV of the *Odyssey,* Odysseus describes the bitter cold and snow that descended on a night foray in which he took part. And, then, the whole point of the Hyperboreans is that they live beyond Boreas, where his chill breath cannot disturb them.]

Hyperion

A Titan, son of Uranus and Gaea and, by Thea, father of Helios (the sun), Selene (the moon), and Eos (the dawn). Hyperion was conceived of as being of radiant and matchless beauty and splendor. [Hamlet says bitterly that his father was to his uncle as "Hyperion to a satyr."]

See HELIOS, APOLLO.

Hypermnestra

The only one of the fifty daughters of Danaus who disobeyed her father and did not kill her husband on their wedding night.

See DANAUS, AEGYPTUS.

Hypnos

The god of sleep. Son of Nyx and brother of death (Thanatos), and father of Morpheus, Icelus, and Phantasus, bringers of various sorts of dreams. He is represented as a winged youth who touches the heads of the tired with a branch, or pours a soporific liquid over them from a horn.

Hypsipyle

Daughter of Thoas, king of Lemnos. The women of Lemnos had neglected the rites of Aphrodite and were punished by the goddess by being given an odor so foul that their husbands would have nothing to do with them. In retaliation the women murdered all of the men—except Thoas, whom Hypsipyle, a devoted daughter, managed to hide and then secretly to convey out of the country. She became queen. The Argonauts visited Lemnos and—either having more robust affections than the ladies' husbands or more obtuse perceptions—mated with them. Hypsipyle had two sons by Jason.

[Certain industrious savants have suggested that the women of Lemnos may have been using the dye woad, which —they assert—has a strongly repulsive odor. But this is being oversubtle: the Germanic tribes used woad extensively as a cosmetic and propagated vigorously. And Aphrodite would have understood woad. But neglected rites are another matter. The story is a nice illustration of the practical nature of much Greek mythology.]

Hyrrokkin

A giant ogress in Norse mythology. She alone had strength enough to launch the death ship on which Balder's funeral pyre was lighted and which conveyed his body and that of his faithful wife Nanna out to sea—where it sank and bore them down to Hel.

Iapetus

A Titan, son of Uranus and Gaea. Father of Prometheus, Epimetheus, and Atlas. Zeus confined him to Tartarus after the defeat of the Titans.

Iasion

Son of Zeus and Electra, he was associated with Demeter. She bore him a child, Plutus, a personification of wealth.

Ibycus, The Cranes of

Ibycus, a poet journeying to a musical contest at Corinth, was murdered by robbers in a grove. As he fell he called out to a flock of cranes passing overhead to avenge him. In the amphitheater later a play was presented in which the avenging Furies were portrayed with a realism that shook the audience. At that moment a flock of cranes flew overhead and one of the murderers (both of whom were in the audience) cried out in terror, "Look, comrade, the avengers of Ibycus!" and by this means revealed their guilt. They were apprehended, confessed, and were executed.

Icarius

An Athenian who had embraced the worship of Dionysus and sought to convert others by giving them wine. Unused to wine, his guests thought they had been poisoned and killed him. His daughter ERIGONE, overcome with grief, hanged herself.

Icarus

See DAEDALUS.

Ida

1. The mountain in Asia Minor on which Paris gave his fatal judgment and, by assigning the apple of discord to Aphrodite, gained Helen as his wife but precipitated the Trojan War. This mountain was the center of the cult of Cybele.
2. The highest mountain in Crete. In a cave on the mountainside the infant Zeus was secretly reared, suckled by a she-goat, his divine mewlings drowned out by the clashing of the shields of the Curetes.

Idas

Son of Aphareus, and one of the Argonauts, has two distinctions in Greek mythology:

(1) When Apollo carried off his bride, Marpessa, Zeus—to prevent Apollo and Idas from fighting—let the lady choose between them. She chose Idas.
(2) When Castor and Pollux carried off the daughters of Leucippides, Idas and his brother Lynceus, their cousins, pursued the Dioscuri and fought them. Both of the brothers were killed but not before Idas had killed Castor.

Idomeneus

King of Crete, grandson of Minos. He fought on the side of the Greeks in the Trojan War. On the way home his ship was caught in a storm and he vowed to sacrifice to Poseidon the first thing that met him on his return home. It happened to be his son. He kept his vow, but the gods sent a pestilence to scourge Crete to atone for this unnatural act and Idomeneus was forced to flee.

[The capricious gods had *not* expressed any uncontrollable indignation at the sacrifice of IPHIGENIA. No more than did Jehovah at the sacrifice by Jephthah (Judges, 11).]

Idunn

The goddess in Norse mythology who kept the apples of youth, the eating of which kept the Aesir forever young. She was carried off by the storm Jotun Tjasse but was brought back by Loki. She was the wife of Bragi.

Igraine (or Igerne, Ygerne)

Wife of Duke (or King) Gorlois of Cornwall, in the Arthurian legends. She was true to her husband but MERLIN managed to make UTHER PENDRAGON assume the exact semblance of Gorlois. Of this union Arthur was born. After the death of Gorlois, Uther Pendragon married Igraine.

Iliad

An account in twenty-four books—commonly ascribed to Homer—largely of the events of the last year of the siege of Troy by the Greeks under Agamemnon.

Calchas, a seer, declares that a plague which has broken out in the Grecian camp can be stopped only by returning to her father (a priest of Apollo) the Trojan maiden Chryseis, who has been claimed by AGAMEMNON. Agamemnon reluctantly consents but recompenses himself by taking, in her place, the maid Briseis, who had been awarded to ACHILLES. This angers Achilles, who retires to his tent and takes his special troops, the MYRMIDONS, out of the battle. The Greek army is beaten back and Agamemnon sues for forgiveness. But Achilles is obdurate until his friend Patroclus (wearing Achilles' armor) is killed by HECTOR. Achilles, wild with grief, re-enters the fight, kills Hector and drags his body in vindictive triumph around the walls of Troy. Priam, king of Troy and Hector's aged father, comes to beg for his son's body, that it may be given due burial rites. And Achilles, his anger spent and his heart moved to pity, grants the request.

At this point the *Iliad* ends and other incidents of the end of Troy—such as the use of the TROJAN HORSE and the sacking of the city—are known to us from post-Homeric sources.

Ilus

Son of Tros and father of Laomedon. He was the founder of Ilium (Troy).

Imhotep

In Egyptian mythology a sage and healer who came to form a triad with Ptah and Sekhmet. In this personification he was regarded as the god of knowledge, and as the patron of medicine was identified by the Greeks with Aesculapius.

Inachus

God of the river Inachus and father of Io. Poseidon and Hera made him the judge of their conflicting claims to Argos. He decided in favor of Hera, and Poseidon dried up his river. Greek mythology has a number of stories (such as that of the Judgment of Paris) in which a mortal or lesser deity is called on to judge a dispute between the gods. Whatever the decision, the loser always persecutes the judge.

INO

Ino

See ATHAMAS.

Inuus

The Roman equivalent of the Greek god Pan. Inuus, however, was particularly the god of fertility among the herds.

Io

Daughter of Inachus, beloved by Zeus, who, in order to conceal her from jealous Hera, changed her into a heifer. Hera set Argus, the hundred-eyed monster, to watch her (presumably so that she could not be changed back into human form) and Zeus sent Hermes to kill Argus. Hera then had Io tormented by a gadfly that drove her to swim across the Ionian sea to Egypt. There she resumed her human form (though in her representations—and probably in assimilation with Hathor—she retained a cow's head) and bore a son, Epaphus.

Iole

See DEIANIRA, IPHITUS.

Ion

See CREUSA 1.

Iphicles

The twin brother of Hercules. They had the same mother, Alcmene, and were born at the same time. But Hercules' father was Zeus; Iphicles' father was Amphitryon (whose semblance Zeus had assumed in begetting Hercules). Hercules, in his madness, killed two of his brother's children.

Iphigenia

The daughter of Agamemnon and Clytemnestra. Agamemnon had offended the goddess Artemis (various reasons for the offense are given in various versions of the legend) and she held the Grecian fleet, bound for Troy, at Aulis with contrary winds, demanding, in expiation, that Agamemnon sacrifice his daughter. The girl was sent for on the pretext that she was to marry Achilles, but instead was sacrificed. In the *Agamemnon* of Aeschylus this was one of the reasons for Clytemnestra's bitter hatred of her husband.

In another version of her story Iphigenia was not actually sacrificed but carried away by Artemis in a cloud while a stag or some other creature was substituted for her. She was taken to Tauris, where she became a priestess of Artemis. To Tauris, eventually, came her brother, Orestes, and his friend Pylades, seeking to carry off to Greece the Taurian image of Artemis (as a necessary prelude to freeing Orestes from the persecution of the Erinyes). The Taurians would have killed them but Iphigenia helped them escape with the image.

Iphis

A young Cypriot who loved a lady, Anaxarete, who did not love him. He hanged himself at her door while she looked on in cheerful indifference. Aphrodite turned her into stone.

Iphitus

Son of Eurytus and hence brother of Iole *(see* HERCULES). As a friend of Hercules, he favored the hero's suit for his sister's hand in marriage. But Eurytus would not allow the marriage, even though Hercules had won her by his success in archery (the required test). In a fit of madness at this rejection, Hercules killed Iphitus—for which act he was condemned to spend three years as a slave of Queen OMPHALE.

Iris

Goddess of the rainbow. She sometimes served as a messenger for the goddess Hera.

Irus

An insolent beggar in the *Odyssey* who insulted the disguised Odysseus as he returned to his palace at Ithaca. Egged on by the suitors, Irus challenged Odysseus to a fight and the angry hero felled him with a single blow, breaking his jaw. It was, however, a dangerous gratification of a moment's resentment, since it might have suggested to men less assured than the suitors that the disguised Odysseus was not the feeble old beggar he seemed to be.

Ishtar

The Babylonian goddess of love and fertility. She was the wife of Tammuz and when he died she descended into the underworld to bring him back.

Isis

The chief female deity of Egyptian mythology, the wife of Osiris and the mother of Horus. Her cult was widespread throughout Greece and Rome.

Islands of the Blest

See ELYSIUM.

Ismene

Daughter of Oedipus and Jocasta, sister of Eteocles, Polynices, and Antigone. When Creon forbids the burial of

Polynices, Antigone, at the cost of her life, defies this impious command. Ismene, lacking her sister's force of character, though shocked at the treatment of her brother's body, is equally shocked at Antigone's defiance and will not help her. Antigone scorns her weak sister and will not even permit her later to claim she had a part in the deed.

Isolde (or Isoud)

1. Of Ireland.
2. Of the White Hands.
   See TRISTRAM.

Itylus (or Itys)

See AËDON, PHILOMELA.

Itys

See PHILOMELA.

Iulus

Another—later—name for young Ascanius, the son of Aeneas.

Ixion

King of the Lapithae. He agreed to marry Dia, daughter of Eioneus, and promised her father rich bridal gifts. However, he avoided payment of these by luring Eioneus into a concealed pit filled with burning charcoal.

Despite this, Zeus took a liking to him and even brought him to eat at the celestial table on Olympus—a gracious favor which the wretch repaid by planning to seduce Hera!

IXION

But Zeus substituted a cloud for Hera and upon the cloud Ixion begot the Centaurs. To punish him for such unparalleled presumption and ingratitude, Zeus had him bound to a fiery wheel which turns forever.

Jamshid

A king in Zoroastrian mythology who reigned seven hundred years, a feat made possible by his obtaining—with the help of the Genii—the elixir of life, which he drank from a seven-ringed cup. He finally met an unpleasant end, being sawed in two by Dashak.

> [Iram indeed is gone with all his Rose,
> And Jamshyd's Seven-ringed Cup where no one knows.
>
> And this first Summer month that brings the Rose
> Shall take Jamshyd and Kaikobád away.
>
> They say the Lion and the Lizard keep
> The Courts where Jamshyd gloried and drank deep.
>
> —Edward Fitzgerald, *The Rubaiyat of Omar Khayyam*]

Janus

The Roman god with two faces who guarded doors and who, in consequence, became the god of entries or beginnings. From the first of these concepts comes our word *janitor;*

from the second, *January*. The two faces did not—as in the modern expression—imply duplicity, but vigilance.

It was a peculiarity of this god that the doors of his temple were kept open in time of war and closed in time of universal peace. They were rarely closed.

Jason

Son of Aeson and leader of the ARGONAUTS. His uncle, Pelias, unlawfully withheld the throne of Thessaly from Jason but promised to surrender it when the young hero brought him the GOLDEN FLEECE from Colchis. Jason had a great ship, the *Argo,* built and collected a band of heroes, the Argonauts, who sailed with him. After many adventures and with the assistance of MEDEA, daughter of Aeëtes, king of Colchis, Jason seized the fleece and managed to escape with it. Medea accompanied him, rejuvenated his old father by her magic skills, and treacherously killed King Pelias.

This last act compelled them to flee from Thessaly and Jason took refuge with Creon, king of Corinth, whose daughter, Glauce (also called *Creusa),* he sought in marriage, planning to cast Medea off. Medea, enraged, killed Glauce and Creon and, to be particularly revenged on Jason, killed her own children by him. She then fled in a dragon chariot to Athens, where she married King Aegeus.

In his old age Jason was killed by the falling prow of the rotting *Argo,* which had been drawn up on the beach and under which he happened to be sitting.

Jinn

See DJINN.

Jocasta

Queen of Thebes. Daughter of Menoeceus, wife of King Laius, mother and ill-fated, unwitting wife of OEDIPUS. On the revelation of her relation to Oedipus, she hanged herself.

Homer calls her *Epicaste*.

Jord

Daughter of Night and a giantess, she is the wife of ODIN and the mother of THOR.

Jörmungand (or Midgard Serpent)

Begotten by LOKI on the giantess Angurboda and thrown into the sea by Odin, it grew until it encircled the earth, holding its tail in its mouth. Thor once mistook a segment of the creature for a cat and almost pulled its tail out of its mouth attempting to lift it *(see* SKRYMIR). At Ragnarok it will be killed by Thor's hammer, but Thor will drown in its venom.

Jotunheim

The home of the Frost Giants in Norse mythology.

Jotuns

The Frost Giants who ruled before the AESIR. Most of them were violent, wicked, hostile.

See also TROLLS.

Judgment of Paris

See PARIS.

Juno

The Roman goddess of marriage, the home, and childbirth who by virtue of these attributes, and of being the consort of Jupiter, was identified with the Greek Hera.

Jupiter (also called **Jove,** analogue of Greek **Zeus**)

The supreme deity in Roman mythology. He was a sky god, the god of rain (Jupiter Pluvius), and the hurler of the thunderbolt (Jupiter Lapis). Any place struck by lightning was sacred to him. He was the guardian of property, the guarantor of oaths. He was identified with the Greek Zeus; indeed, the first syllable of his name is probably *Zeu(s)*.

Juventas

The Roman analogue of the Greek Hebe, the goddess of youth.

Kali

The wife of Shiva in Vedic mythology. She has many names and is generally represented as dancing and trampling on the body of her husband. She has four hands. One holds a sword, one a human head, one is raised in a gesture of peace, and one in a threatening grasp. She was the goddess of the Thugs, religious fanatics who, as a part of worshipping her, strangled travelers.

Kay

Sir Kay, one of the knights of the Round Table in Malory's *Morte d'Arthur,* a brave knight but disagreeable. He was the son of Sir Ector and served as King Arthur's seneschal.

Keres

Evil, polluting spirits in Greek mythology. Sometimes identified with the Harpies, at other times with the Furies.

Kore

See PERSEPHONE.

Kratos (or **Cratus**)

Son of the Titan Pallas (not to be confused with Pallas Athena) and the river Styx. His name means "strength."

KRIEMHILD

Kriemhild (or **Krimhild**)

The wife of Siegfried in the *Nibelungenlied*. He gave her the
gold of the Nibelungs, for which gold he was later murdered.
She avenged his death but was herself killed.

Labyrinth

The structure that Daedalus built for Minos, king of Crete, as a prison, or compound, for the Minotaur. Its design was so complicated that no one, once entered into it, could find his way out. Theseus was the single exception, and he found his way out, after slaying the Minotaur, only by following the clew of thread which Ariadne had given him.

See ARIADNE, DAEDALUS, MINOS 2, THESEUS.

Lachesis

One of the FATES, or *Moerae* (Roman *Parcae*). She is the one who measures the thread of life.

Ladon

1. The river on whose banks Hercules, after a year's pursuit, captured the CERYNEAN STAG.
2. The dragon, son of Phorcys and Ceto, that guarded the GOLDEN APPLES OF THE HESPERIDES. Hera was very fond of her dragon and wept bitterly when Hercules killed him. She set him in the sky as the Serpent.

LADY OF THE LAKE

Lady of the Lake

See NINEVE.

Laertes

The father of Odysseus. We find him in the *Odyssey* as an old man retired to his farm, too enfeebled to resist or even to protest against the insolence of the suitors who are wasting Odysseus' estate, insulting Penelope, and planning to murder Telemachus. At the last stand against the kinsmen of the slain suitors, Laertes put on his armor once more and cried out with an old warrior's delight to see his son and his son's son vying in valor.

There is a nice touch in the same scene in which Odysseus identifies himself to his father by naming the trees in the orchard which his father had planted and which he had given Odysseus when he was but a child "asking for everything."

[The concluding scenes of the *Odyssey* which show Laertes in his retirement suggest that a kingship in ancient Greece did not always require the death of the holder to pass to another. Here, apparently, the full power had been peacefully handed on to Odysseus at least twenty years before.]

Laestrygones

Cannibal giants who live in a land to the north where "the extremes of day and night so nearly meet" that the shepherd going out with his flocks meets his fellow shepherd coming in. Odysseus, in an evil hour, came to their land and they ate many of his men.

Laius

King of Thebes. Father and victim of Oedipus. Laius had kidnapped Chrysippos, the young son of Pelops—an act of special wickedness because Pelops had befriended him—and this sin was the cause of the curse on his line.

Lamia

An evil spirit that steals and kills children. Originally Lamia was a queen in Libya. She was loved by Zeus, and Hera, jealous, killed all of Lamia's children. Lamia (helpless against Hera) avenges herself by destroying other people's children. She was thought to have the form of a serpent and in time came to be used as a bogey with which to frighten children. Keats' poem *Lamia* retells an old story of a man who, unwittingly, married a lamia.

Laocoön

Son of Priam and priest of Apollo. Having offended Apollo (in one account) by marrying, or Athena (in another account) by opposing the acceptance of the Wooden Horse *(see* TROJAN HORSE) within the walls of Troy, he and his two sons were strangled by two great serpents.

[The scene, depicted in marble, is one of the best known of all antique sculptures. Lessing, the German critic, used the sculpture as a text for his epoch-making essay on the limits of art (1760).]

Laodamia

Wife of Protesilaus. He was killed at the very disembarkation of the Greek army as they arrived before Troy. His wife begged the gods to be allowed to have three hours with him before he descended to the underworld. Her wish was granted and when the three hours had passed she chose to go with him to Hades rather than to remain in the upper world without him. The story is the subject of a poem by Wordsworth.

LAOMEDON

Laomedon

The father of Priam. He was the founder of Troy. Poseidon helped to build the city for him but Laomedon, once the walls were built, refused to pay Poseidon what he had promised him and, in consequence, was required to chain his daughter Hesione to a rock where she would be seized or devoured by a sea monster. Hercules freed her on the promise of a pair of supernatural horses which Laomedon possessed. But again the monarch refused payment and Hercules killed Laomedon and all of his sons except Priam.

Lapithae

A Thessalian people, subjects of King PIRITHOUS. On the occasion of Pirithous' marriage to Hippodameia the Centaurs (who were related to the king) were invited. One of them, drunk, attempted to carry off the bride and a fierce struggle ensued, a struggle in which the Centaurs were eventually defeated and driven off. The incident is depicted on the Parthenon.

Lares and Penates

The Roman household gods. They watched over the household and its members. Food was offered to them at every meal and rites paid on special occasions set aside for them. The chief of them, the Lar, was the spirit of the founder of the family. The Penates (literally = "those who live in the cupboard") were more personifications of those qualities that would protect and foster the welfare of the family.

[*Lares and Penates* is often used today to designate those familiar objects of which in time we have grown so fond that we could not conceive of it being our home without them.]

Larvae

The ancient Roman name for evil spirits and ghosts. Suetonius says that the *Larva* of the Emperor Caligula was seen after his death.

[From meaning a spectre, the word came to mean a mask and then a "disguised" or masked insect.]

Latinus

King of Latium, in central Italy, who gave his daughter Lavinia as a wife to Aeneas.

See LAVINIA.

Latona

The Roman name for the Greek LETO, the mother of Apollo and Artemis by Zeus.

Laudegreaunce (or **Leodegraunce**)

Father of Guinevere, hence King Arthur's father-in-law. He gave Arthur the Round Table.

Launcelot of the Lake

The most famous of the knights of King Arthur's Round Table. He was the son of King Ban of Brittany, stolen as a child by the Lady of the Lake and brought by her to Arthur's court when he reached manhood. He and Queen Guinevere become lovers and his code thereafter compels him to be true to her while being false to Arthur, his liege lord ["His honour rooted in dishonour stood,/ And faith unfaithful kept him falsely true"—Tennyson, *Lancelot and Elaine*].

They are betrayed to the king by Agravain, and Arthur, with twelve knights, surprises the lovers. Launcelot kills eleven of the knights—all but Modred, escapes, and carries

LAUNFAL

off Guinevere. He restores her to Arthur and retires to Brittany, where Arthur and Gawain attack him. Launcelot wounds Gawain. Modred seizes the kingdom. In the ensuing fighting Gawain is killed and Arthur and Modred fatally wound each other. Launcelot returns to help Arthur but arrives too late. Guinevere has taken the veil and Launcelot becomes a priest and guards Arthur's grave. On his death he is (apparently) received into heaven.

Launfal

A knight of the Round Table (though not mentioned in Malory's *Morte d'Arthur*). He leaves the corrupt court and lives in poverty. Tryamon, a fairy princess, loves him and gives him wealth on condition that he is not to reveal their love. At Arthur's court (to which he returns) Guinevere loves him but he rejects her, boasting that he loves a more beautiful lady. This boast violates his promise to Tryamon and all his wealth disappears. He is required to produce the beautiful lady, and at the trial Tryamon appears, supports his boast, and blinds Guinevere.

[The Launfal of James Russell Lowell's *The Vision of Sir Launfal* (1848) has no relation to the Launfal of Thomas Chestre or Marie de France, the medieval romancers. In this poem—known to every American schoolboy two generations ago—the haughty knight, riding forth in search of the Grail throws a piece of gold to a leper, who scorns the gift. After years of fruitlessly seeking the Grail, Sir Launfal returns many years later, re-encounters the leper and shares with him his last crust, and offers him water to drink from his bowl. The leper turns out to be Christ, the bowl the long-sought-for Grail, and the moral: "Who gives himself with his alms feeds three:/ Himself, his hungering neighbor, and me."]

Lavinia

Daughter of Latinus, king of the Latini. She was betrothed to Turnus, king of the Rutuli, but abandoned him at the behest of an oracle and married Aeneas. Turnus was killed by Aeneas in single combat. Amata, her mother, committed suicide.

Leander

See Hero and Leander.

Leda

Wife of Tyndareus of Sparta and mother of Helen, Clytemnestra, Castor, and Pollux. Helen was the daughter of Zeus, who approached Leda in the form of a swan. Some legends state that the Dioscuri (Castor and Pollux) were sons of Tyndareus, others that Pollux was the son of Zeus and Castor of Tyndareus.

Lemnos

A large island in the Aegean sea onto which Hephaestus fell after Zeus had thrown him from heaven for interfering in a family quarrel between his parents (Zeus and Hera). Hephaestus established his smithy and workshop on Lemnos.

Lemnos had another distinction. The women of the island offended the goddess Aphrodite by neglecting her due rites and she, to punish them, gave them an offensive odor. Their husbands neglected them, finding more odoriferous bedmates in some captured Thracian women. The Lemnian women then murdered their husbands and their race would have died out had not the lusty—and, apparently, unfinicky—Argonauts come along and replenished the population.

LETHE

[It is astonishing that the cosmetic industry has not exploited this incident in their advertising.]

Lethe

The river of oblivion, one of the five rivers of the underworld in Greek mythology.

Leto (Latin Latona)

A Titaness, daughter of Coeus and Phoebe, and mother, by Zeus, of Apollo and Artemis.

Leucothea

The name assumed by INO (see also ATHAMAS) after she had been changed to a sea nymph. In the *Odyssey* she helps the shipwrecked Odysseus reach the island of Scheria, where he is succored by the hospitable Phaeacians.

Lichas

The friend of Hercules who innocently bore to him—from Deianira—the poisoned shirt of Nessus. In his death agonies Hercules hurled Lichas into the sea.

Lidskjalf

Odin's throne, from which he could see the entire world.

Lilith

In Isaiah 34:14 she appears as a night demon. In rabbinical tradition, she was Adam's first wife.

Limnades

Nymphs of lakes, marshes, and swamps. They mislead travelers by crying for help.

Litai

Pleasant goddesses whose amiable function was to recompense those whom Ate (the goddess of rash impulses) had ruined. Like Ate, they were thought of as daughters of Zeus. They were represented as lame, wrinkled, and squinting— conditions caused by all the trouble Ate put them to.

Lodur

Brother of ODIN. He is sometimes called *Ve*. When the first man and woman were created he gave them their senses.

Lohengrin

Son of Parsifal and knight of the Holy Grail. In a swan-drawn boat he rescues Elsa of Brabant. They marry but he is compelled to leave her when she violates an agreement and asks him his name.

Loki

The Norse god of evil and destruction. By birth Loki was not one of the Aesir but a Jotun, but a strange Jotun in that he was handsome and well mannered. So much so that Odin (presumably *before* he had acquired wisdom from YGGDRASIL, MIRMIR's head, and the VOLVA) adopted him as a blood brother. And this, by Old Norse custom, made him a full member of the Aesir and rendered him free from attack by the other gods no matter what he did. And he was full of malicious mischief and was basically evil.

By the giantess Angurboda he sired Jörmungand (the Midgard Serpent), Fenrir (the terrible wolf that, at Ragnarok, will swallow the sun), and Hel (queen of the dead). By the stallion SVALDIFARI he was *mother* to Sleipnir, Odin's eight-legged horse, and although his luring the stallion away from his task

LOKI

saved Asgärd, his bearing the foal caused him to be held in contempt among the super-masculine valiants of Valhalla.

It was Loki who tricked the blind Hoder into throwing the sprig of mistletoe that killed Balder. And it was Loki, disguised as the hateful crone Thokk, who would not weep for Balder dead and hence prevented him from returning from Hel. For this and other evil deeds he was bound in a cave by the other gods, who set over him a serpent from whose jaws there dripped a poisonous venom. When the venom strikes his face it causes him frightful pain, but most of the time it is caught in a cup by his faithful Aesir wife Signe (or Sigun), who watches over him. When she must turn aside, however, to empty the cup, the venom falls on him and he writhes with such violent anguish that it causes earthquakes.

At Ragnarok he will be freed and he and HEIMDAL will kill each other.

[Loki is a fascinating figure. In the Old Testament (Job 1–2) Satan is shown as consorting with God and the angels, sneering, doubting, and being generally disagreeable. But he is plainly God's agent and under God's complete control. In the New Testament he has far more power and has legions of subordinates, but there is still no doubt of his inferiority or of the fact that he exists only on sufferance. In Greek mythology, Zeus is likewise supreme. There is a great deal of squabbling and undignified conduct among the gods, endless jealousies, and petty rivalries. There is even a plot among them to overthrow Zeus but when, at Zeus' command, Briareus rises from the deep, the plot collapses. The Greek gods are childlike, petty and impulsive and vindictive. But they are not *evil* and can cause suffering only to human beings and, even then, only to such and to the extent that Zeus (or Fate) permits.

But Loki *is* evil, the more evil for being subtle and clever.

And his evilness will contribute heavily to the utter destruction of the gods and of the world because he is, actually, a Jotun—in reality the most successful of the Jotuns, for he is also one of the gods. And in the realization, which Loki personifies, as it were, that evil is inextricably intertwined with good, that the two are, indeed, often indistinguishable, and that good by its very goodness, its generosity, its sense of honor, its keeping its word even to its own disadvantage, contributes to its own destruction—in this there is a strength in Norse mythology, for all its innocence and naivete, which makes it in some respects superior, in its poetic insight, to Greek or Christian beliefs.]

Lot

King of Orkney, he married Morgause, one of the daughters of UTHER PENDRAGON and sister of King Arthur. Lot is the leader of Arthur's enemies.

[Lot may be the King Lludd of British mythology, the *Lud* of Ludgate Hill.]

Lotus-Eaters (Lotophagi)

A people upon whom Odysseus and his men came after they had escaped the murderous Ciconians and had survived a prolonged tempest.

The Lotus-Eaters "browsed on a food of flowers" of some narcotic plant, a diet which induced a dreamy lassitude, a soporific contentment and freedom from care. Some of Odysseus' men ate of this food and immediately lost all desire to return to Ithaca and wished to remain in the land of the Lotus-Eaters forever. Odysseus had these men dragged back to the ship by main force and "bound beneath the benches" until they had gained the open sea.

LOXIAS

[Tennyson made this incident the subject of one of his greatest mood poems, *The Lotos-Eaters*:

> In the afternoon they came unto a land
> In which it seemed always afternoon.
> All round the coast the languid air did swoon,
> Breathing like one that hath a weary dream.]

Loxias

Meaning "crooked" or "ambiguous," *Loxias* was an epithet applied to the god Apollo in special reference to his oracle at Delphi. The term did not suggest a reprehensible deviousness in the god—especially since he was as the oracle merely the mouthpiece of Zeus—but stressed his mysteriousness and inscrutability.

Lucina

The Roman goddess of childbirth.

Lucius

A Roman emperor in Malory's *Morte d'Arthur* against whom Arthur wages war. Lucius is assisted by giants and Saracens, but after many battles and individual contests he is defeated and Arthur is crowned in Rome.

Lucretia

Shakespeare's *Lucrece*. She was the wife of Tarquinius Collatinus and was raped by Tarquinius Sextus. Because of this act the Tarquins were expelled from Rome and a republic replaced their kingdom.

Luna

The Roman goddess of the moon, analogue of the Greek SELENE.

Lycaon

King of Arcadia. Zeus visited him in disguise but he was suspicious of his guest's identity and to test it offered him a meal of human flesh. Zeus, to punish this impiety, struck Lycaon's sons with a thunderbolt and changed Lycaon into a wolf. Some versions state that it was because of Lycaon's spectacular wickedness (among other things, he tried to murder Zeus!) that Zeus produced the deluge which Deucalion and his wife Pyrrha alone survived.

Lycomedes

King of Scyros. It was at his court that the young Achilles was kept, disguised as a girl, his mother Thetis having preferred for him (she had been offered the choice) a long life of quiet obscurity to a short life of military glory. His disguise was exposed by Odysseus, who penetrated the court as a merchant trader and cunningly exposed a splendid suit of armor while having trumpets sound the call to arms.

Lycomedes achieved sinister fame by pushing his guest, the exiled Theseus, off a cliff.

Lycurgus

King of the Edones. He opposed the worship of Dionysus and the god drove him mad. In his madness he killed his son, thinking him to be a vine plant. Regaining his sanity, he committed suicide.

LYNCEUS

Lynceus

1. Fortunate husband of Hypermnestra—she being the only one of the fifty DANAÏDES who did not murder her husband on their wedding night.

2. One of the Argonauts. Also took part in the Calydonian Boar Hunt. As his name implies, he was gifted with supernaturally keen sight. He was the son of Aphareus and the brother of Idas. The brothers were about to marry the daughters of Leucippus when Castor and Pollux carried off the brides and killed the grooms.

Lyones

The Lady of the Castle Perilous in the Arthurian legend. Sir Gareth rescues and marries her.

Machaon

Son of Aesculapius. Surgeon and physician of the Grecian army during the Trojan War. His most famous and influential case was the healing of PHILOCTETES. Healed of his presumably incurable wound, the great archer lent his skill and his invincible bow to the Grecian cause.

Maenads (also called **Bacchae** or **Thyiades**)

The frenzied women who celebrated the rites of Dionysus with uninhibited fury, destroying all who opposed or declined their wild rites, indulging in fierce orgies, etc., especially with satyrs and sileni. With their bare hands they tore to pieces PENTHEUS and ORPHEUS.

Maera

See ERIGONE.

Maia

The most beautiful of the PLEIADS and the mother of Hermes (by Zeus). She became a fertility goddess and blended with the great Phrygian goddess Cybele and the Roman Bona Dea.

MANES

Manes

The spirits of the dead. Unless propitiated or appeased by due rites or the fulfillment of obligations, the manes might become vindictive.

Marduk

The chief of the Babylonian gods. Like the Greek and the Norse gods, the Babylonian gods had to fight to secure their power. Their chief enemy was TIAMAT. As the storm god, Marduk controlled the winds and slew Tiamat by forcing so violent a wind down her throat that she burst.

Mark

King of Cornwall, uncle of TRISTRAM and husband of Isolde of Ireland—in the Arthurian legends.

Marpessa

Daughter of Evenus, a river god, and Alcippe. She was beloved by Apollo, who promised her immortality, and by Idas, "that was strongest of men that were then of Earth." Zeus allowed her to choose—and she chose an earthly lover and all the joys and sorrows of mortality.

Mars

The Roman analogue of the Greek ARES. Exalting military power and glory, the Romans exalted Mars to one of the chief gods of their pantheon, whereas the Greeks saw him as a blustering and brutal coward and one of the least likable of the gods. The Greeks gave a loftier place to Athena, the armed goddess of wisdom. But with her, wisdom always dominated the arms.

Marsyas

A satyr. He picked up the flutes which Athena had thrown away (because flute-playing distorted her face and made her appear undignified) and the goddess had beaten him for his impertinence. Unable to take even a celestial hint, apparently, he challenged Apollo to a contest of musical skill and Apollo had him flayed alive.

Mead

Drink of the Norse gods, flowing in limitless profusion from the udder of the goat Heidrun.

Medea

Daughter of Aeëtes, king of Colchis, and Eidyia, his queen. Through her mother, Medea was grand-daughter of Helios and niece of Circe. When the Argonauts came to Colchis to obtain the GOLDEN FLEECE, Medea, who had fallen in love with Jason, enabled them, through her magic, to accomplish their task and escape with the fleece. They were pursued by Aeëtes, but Medea effected their flight by cutting her young brother Absyrtus into pieces and scattering the pieces behind them as they fled. Aeëtes stopped to pick up the pieces and Jason and Medea got away.

Back in Iolcus she renewed the youth of Jason's father but by a ruse tricked the daughters of Pelias (Jason's half brother who was wrongfully keeping him from the throne) into killing their father. When Jason was unfaithful to her and sought to replace her as his wife with Glauce, the daughter of King Creon, she murdered Glauce and, to spite Jason, his and her own children as well. From this situation she escaped to Athens, where she was protected by—and married to—King Aegeus, to whom she bore Medus, the ancestor of the

MEDON

Medes. Her attempts to get him to kill Perseus, his son—though he did not at first recognize him as such—strained their relations and Aegeus drove her out. But because she had repulsed the advances of Zeus, Hera made her immortal and in the underworld she married Achilles.

[One of the earliest of militant feminists!]

Medon

Penelope's faithful herald who, in the *Odyssey*, tells her of the suitors' plot to kill Telemachus. At the killing of the suitors he is spared.

Medusa

See GORGONS, PEGASUS, AEGIS.

Magaera

One of the EUMENIDES.

Megara

1. The country over which King NISUS ruled.
2. Hercules' first wife. She and her children were killed by him in a fit of insanity into which the implacable Hera had driven him. In expiation he performed the Twelve Labors.

See HERCULES.

Melampus

A soothsayer who—in consquence of serpents having licked his ears—understood the speech of all living things. He was imprisoned by Iphiclus (whose cattle he was attempting to steal) but was freed when (having overheard the talk of some worms) he foretold the collapse of the roof. By his magic he removed the curse of sterility from Iphiclus and all was forgiven.

Melanippus

One of the defenders of Thebes against the Seven, he fought and fatally wounded Tydeus but was himself killed in the encounter. Tydeus, dying, asked for Melanippus' head and when it was brought to him bit it savagely. This act so horrified the gods that they immediately abandoned their intention of making Tydeus immortal.

Melanthius

A goatherd who is disloyal to his absent master, Odysseus, and supports the suitors. He is killed in the general slaughter of Odysseus' vengeance.

Melantho

A disloyal maid in Odysseus' palace at Ithaca. He drives her and the other serving girls who are insolent and partial to the suitors from the hall and later kills them.

Meleager

Son of Oeneus of Calydon and Althaea. He was one of the Argonauts and it was he who killed the Calydonian Boar. When he was a newborn baby it was revealed to his mother that he would die as soon as a log then burning on the hearth was consumed. Althaea snatched the log from the hearth, extinguished the flames that were burning it, and hid it away, wrapped in a cloth. Years later when Meleager in a quarrel had killed her brothers she threw the log back into a fire and let it be burned up.

MELICERTES

Melicertes

Infant son of INO who was transformed into the sea god Palaemon when his frantic mother (fleeing from her mad husband, Athamas) leaped with her child into the sea.

Melpomene

The Muse of tragedy.

Memeros and Pheres

The children whom Medea killed in order to be revenged on Jason for abandoning her for Glauce.

[This story is fairly late; Euripides was the first to tell it.]

Memnon

Son of Eos and TITHONUS. He fought on the Trojan side in the Trojan War and was killed by Achilles. However Zeus made him immortal and he was worshipped in Ethiopia, where he had been a king. The statue of Amenophis at Thebes was thought by the Greeks to be a statue of Memnon and it was believed that when it was struck by the rays of the rising sun, it produced a sound, a musical twang, like the breaking of the string of a lyre. And this was interpreted as Eos, the dawn, eternally lamenting for her son.

Menelaus

Son of Atreus, brother of Agamemnon and—the most important thing in his myth—the husband of Helen. In the *Iliad* he plays a subordinate role under his great warrior brother. But he does fight a duel with Paris, his wife's abductor, and would have killed him had not Aphrodite magically intervened. He was king of Sparta and in the *Odyssey* is seen, long after the fall of Troy, living in placid domesticity with the reclaimed Helen.

Menoeceus

1. The father of JOCASTA and CREON 1.
2. The son of Creon, king of Thebes, and hence the grandson of Menoeceus 1. The gods revealed, through Tiresias, that Thebes would withstand the assault of the Seven *(see* SEVEN AGAINST THEBES) only if atonement, in the form of a human sacrifice, was made for Cadmus' killing of the dragon. Menoeceus—despite his father's anguished attempt to prevent it—killed himself at the dragon's lair.

Mentor

Wise old friend of Odysseus who remained behind in Ithaca as a counselor to Penelope and tutor to Telemachus. Athena assumed his form when she accompanied Telemachus to Sparta on his search for news of his father. It is in the guise of Mentor, also, that she advises the angry kinsmen of the slain suitors to accept the inevitable and not to plunge Ithaca into civil war.

[*Mentor* has passed into our language as a term for any wise and faithful counselor.]

Mercury

See HERMES.

Merlin

The magician (fathered by the devil on the nun Matilda) who plays a major role in the Arthurian stories. He aids Uther Pendragon in his deceitful seduction of Igraine—which results in the conception of Arthur. It is by his magic that the stones of Stonehenge are assembled. It is Merlin who made the Round Table. He dotes upon the damsel NINEVE, who learns enough magic from him to pinion him forever under a huge rock (or, in other versions, to imprison him within an oak tree).

Merope

1. One of the Pleiads. She is the dimmest of these stars, hiding her head in shame because she had married a mortal while all of her sisters had had affairs with gods.

2. Wife of Polybus and foster mother of Oedipus. When OEDIPUS heard the oracle proclaim that he would marry his mother, he fled from Merope, believing that she was his real mother.

Metis (= "wisdom")

A goddess who was fated to bear Athena to Zeus and then another child more powerful than Zeus himself. To prevent this, Zeus swallowed her. Athena was born from his forehead and Zeus had wisdom eternally within himself.

Midas

A king of Phrygia about whom several legends had collected. Of these, two are far better known than the others:

(1) As judge of a musical contest between Apollo and Pan he declared Pan to be the winner and Apollo, in scorn, gave him the ears of an ass. Midas hid these under his Phrygian cap and no one knew of them except his barber, who was enjoined to secrecy on pain of death. The barber, finding his incommunicable knowledge unbearable, dug a hole in the ground into which he whispered "Midas has the ears of an ass." From the hole grew a tree which, when the wind blew, rustled the statement to the air.

(2) Midas having befriended a persecuted Silenus, Dionysus (granting Midas' own ill-considered request) decreed that anything he touched should turn to gold. But Midas almost immediately found that he could not eat, since his food turned to gold. He was allowed to lose the gift (one of the few instances in Greek mythology of a gift's being revocable) by bathing in the river Pactolus, which, thereafter, had golden sands.

Midgard

Earth, fashioned by Odin and his two brothers from the body of the dead giant Ymir.

Midgard Serpent

See JÖRMUNGAND.

Mimir

A wise, ancient Jotun, friendly to the Aesir. He guarded the well of wisdom that lay under the roots of the life-tree Yggdrasil. He himself had drunk from the well and knew all things —past, present, and future. He allowed Odin to drink from the well but only by paying for the privilege with one of his eyes. Thereafter Odin always wore a lock of hair hanging over the empty socket or, in other accounts, wore a broad-brimmed blue hat (the sky) that concealed his deformity. According to still other accounts Odin, after having read the mystical runes, never smiled again.

There was no resentment against Mimir. He lived among the Aesir and was treated with respect. He was sent as a hostage to the Vanir, who beheaded him. Odin got the head back, breathed life into it and used to consult it on important occasions.

MINERVA

Minerva

See ATHENA.

Minos

1. Son of Zeus and Europa. King of Crete and, after his death, a judge in the underworld.
2. By some reckoned the same as Minos 1, by others as his grandson, also king of Crete. At his request Poseidon sent a bull from the sea to be sacrificed, but the bull was such a splendid creature that Minos did not sacrifice it. Poseidon (in some accounts, Aphrodite) caused Pasiphaë, Minos' wife, to fall in love with the bull and to prevail upon DAEDALUS to construct a cowlike device within which she might gratify her passion. The product of this unnatural union was the Minotaur, a creature with the head of a bull and the body of a man, and which was imprisoned in the Labyrinth that Daedalus constructed to hide it.

Minos made war on Athens and, being victorious, demanded as atonement for the death of his son Androgeus, killed in the war, that the Athenians send him a yearly tribute of young men and young women to be sacrificed to the Minotaur. Theseus slew the Minotaur and freed Athens from this grisly and humiliating tribute. Daedalus escaped by devising wings and flying to Sicily. Minos pursued him but met his death in the house of Cocalus, who was sheltering him. Cocalus pretended to receive Minos with hospitality and had the usual warm bath prepared for him. But the water poured over him in the bath was boiling and fatal.

Minotaur

See MINOS 2, THESEUS, ARIADNE.

Misenos (or **Misenus**)

A trumpeter, mentioned in the sixth book of Vergil's *Aeneid,* who rashly challenged Triton to a competition in trumpet-blowing and was drowned for his presumption by the indignant god.

Mithra (or **Mithras**)

The god of light in ancient Persian mythology. He was a friend to man and a foe of evil. He is commonly depicted as a young man wearing a short tunic and a Phrygian cap and thrusting a sword into the neck of a bull. His worship was widespread in the Roman Empire in the second century A.D. and its rituals affected the forms of Christianity.

Mjolnir (or **Miolnir**)

Thor's magic and devastating hammer (the thunderbolt), which when thrown always returned to his hand. It had been forged by the dwarf Sindri. Loki disguised as a fly tried to interfere with its forging and did bother the dwarf to such an extent that the hammer had a very short handle, but Thor could throw it. Its stroke was fatal, but it was sometimes used to bring the dead back to life and it blessed weddings. Indeed Thursday (Thor's day) was a special day for Norse weddings.

Mnemosyne

The goddess of memory. She was the daughter of Uranus and Gaea and, by Zeus, the mother of the Muses.

Modi

Son of Thor. One of the seven gods to survive Ragnarok.

MODRED

Modred (or Mordred)

Son of King Lot of the Orkneys and of Morgause, King Arthur's sister. Geoffrey of Monmouth represents Modred as Arthur's son by his sister. While Arthur was out of England, fighting the Roman emperor Lucius, Modred treacherously seized the kingdom. He was killed by Arthur in the final battle, but not before he had given Arthur his death wound.

Moerae

See FATES.

Moirai

See FATES.

Moly

A magic herb which Hermes gave to Odysseus on Circe's island to protect him from the witch's power.

Momus

The god of censure and ridicule. He was the son of Night and the brother of Sleep, of Death, of Dreams, and of Care.

Moneta

Meaning, apparently, "the admonisher" or "the one who reminds," this became one of the titles of Juno. There are various explanations, none of them either clear or convincing. What is certain, however, is that the temple dedicated to her under this name became the Roman mint and from that fact comes our word *money*.

Mopsus

1. A seer. One of the Lapithae, son of Ampyx and the nymph Chloris. He took part in the Calydonian Boar Hunt, in the fight between the Lapithae and the Centaurs, and was one of the Argonauts. He died of a snakebite.

2. A seer. Son of the Cretan seer Rhacius and Manto, daughter of Tiresias. Famous for a contest in seermanship with the great seer CALCHAS. Calchas challenged Mopsus to guess the number of figs on a tree and Mopsus (with closed eyes!) got it right, to the very last fig. Then, challenged to guess the time of delivery and the number of pigs in the farrow of a pregnant sow, he was right to the day of farrowing and the number and the sex of the pigs in the farrow, whereas Calchas missed it badly and died of chagrin.

Morgan le Fay

Necromancer daughter of UTHER PENDRAGON, she was educated in a nunnery and later married King Uriens. In one version of the Arthurian stories it is she who reveals to Arthur the illicit love of Launcelot and Queen Guinevere. In Malory's *Morte d'Arthur* she tries to kill Arthur and tries to kill her husband. She is one of the three black-robed women on the mysterious barge in which the wounded Arthur is borne away to Avalon.

Morgause (or Morgawse, Margawse)

Sister of King Arthur, wife of King Lot of Orkney, mother of Modred, Gawain, Agravain, Gaheris, and Gareth.

Morpheus

Though often today spoken of as if he were the god of sleep, Morpheus was actually the son of Hypnos, the god of sleep (Latin *Somnus)* and was the bringer of dreams.

MUSES

Muses

The nine daughters of Zeus and Mnemosyne (memory). They sing and dance at Olympian festivities. The Sirens once tried to compete with them but were ignominiously defeated. Each Muse is now assigned to a special department of the arts. But scholars regard this specialization as a fairly late development; one of the greatest scholars goes so far as to label it "silly and pedantic."

The Muses, as they are commonly designated and assigned are:

Calliope	Muse of epic poetry
Clio	Muse of history
Euterpe	Muse of the flute and Dionysiac music
Thalia	Muse of comedy
Melpomene	Muse of tragedy
Terpsichore	Muse of the dance and lyric poetry
Erato	Muse of lyric poetry, hymns, and erotic poetry
Polyhymnia	Muse of the solemn hymn and religious dance
Urania	Muse of astronomy

Muspellsheim

In Norse mythology a region of fire lying to the south of the abyss Ginnungagap. At Ragnarok, Surtr, a fire giant who rules over Muspellsheim, will lead his followers against the gods and will finally engulf the whole world in flames and utterly consume it.

Myrmidons

The word—which now means those who execute an order, especially a military command, with ruthless indifference to its baseness or inhumanity—derives from the Greek word for *ant*. AEACUS, the pious ruler of the island of Aegina, besought Zeus to replenish the population of the island which had been destroyed by a plague. Zeus turned a swarm of ants into men, but they were men who followed their leader with the furious energy and blind devotion of ants. When Aeacus' grandson, Achilles, went off to the Trojan War his soldiers were drawn from the Myrmidons and distinguished themselves by their efficient savagery.

Nagelfar

A ghastly ship, made from dead men's nails, that at Ragnarok will bring ghosts to the great battle.

[The Norsemen, according to the d'Aulaires, used to cut the nails of the dead just to slow down the supply of materials needed for this ship—and thereby to put off Ragnarok as long as possible.]

Naiads

Nymphs of streams, ponds, and other fresh waters. River nymphs are Naiads but, more strictly, are Potameides.
See also LIMNADES.

Nanna

Wife of Balder and mother of Forseti in Norse mythology. She was burned on her husband's funeral pyre and remained with him in Hel.

Narcissus

A beautiful youth, in Greek mythology, who fell in love with his own reflection in a pool. Unable to do anything more than look at the object of his love, he pined away, died, and was changed into a flower. One version of the story has it that he was punished by this *narcissism* (so called, of course, after him) because of his indifference to the love of the nymph ECHO.

Nauplius

A Greek hero, descendant of Poseidon and one of the Argonauts. To avenge the death of his son PALAMEDES he lit misleading beacons and so wrecked the Grecian fleet on its return voyage from Troy.

Nausicaa

The daughter of Alcinous, king of the Phaeacians. She and her handmaidens found the exhausted Odysseus washed ashore and she instructed him how to get safely to her parents and claim their protection. Alcinous hinted broadly that he would like Odysseus to marry her, but the hero longed to return to his own island.

Nectar

The drink of the gods. Like their food, ambrosia, its taste conferred immortality.

Neleus

Son of Poseidon and father of Nestor.

Nemean Lion

The first of the TWELVE LABORS OF HERCULES was to kill this ferocious beast. It seemed impervious to the shattering blows of his mighty club, so he picked it up and squeezed it to death. Thereafter he wore its skin as a mantle and is usually depicted as wearing it.

NEMESIS

> [My fate cries out
> And makes each petty artery in this body
> As hardy as the Nemean lion's nerve.
> —*Hamlet*, I, iv]

Nemesis

A personification of retribution, especially the retribution visited upon presumptuous or wicked mortals by the gods.

Neoptolemus (also called **Pyrrhus**)

Son of Achilles. After his father's death he was sent for by the Greeks and played a large and sanguinary part in the final sack and destruction of Troy. He was one of the warriors concealed within the TROJAN HORSE. He slew Priam and hurled the child ASTYANAX from the walls of Troy to his death on the rocks below. He married Hermione, daughter of Menelaus and Helen. Things had not gone well with him and he made himself a nuisance at the oracle at Delphi, with his violence, blustering, and demanding, until the Pythoness said "Let us be rid of this troublemaker" and a dutiful attendant stabbed him with one of the sacrificial knives. All in all, one of mythology's most thoroughly disagreeable figures!

[It is as "the hellish Pyrrhus," "o'ersized with coagulate gore," the mere "whiff and wind" of whose fell sword blows down the aged Priam that he appears in *Hamlet* (II, ii). Prince Hamlet had eagerly demanded "a passionate speech" from the First Player and, apparently, Pyrrhus and passion went together in Elizabethan high style.]

Nephele

The cloud resemblance to Hera which Zeus created to deceive IXION when he attempted to rape Hera. Out of this union came the Centaurs.

Neptune

The Italian god of water—of rain and fertility therefrom—who came to be identified with the Greek Poseidon, the god of the sea.

Nereids

The fifty sea-nymph daughters of Nereus and Doris. Most famous among them are Amphitrite (wife of Poseidon), THE-TIS, and GALATEA. The Tritons were the masculine attendants upon Poseidon; the Nereids were the female attendants.

Nereus

A sea god, father of the fifty Nereids. He appears in mythology as an old and very wise creature. In one account of Hercules' obtaining of the Apples of the Hesperides it was Nereus who furnished him with the golden cup of the sun with which he reached the fabled land.

Nessus

A Centaur who ferried people over the river Evenus. Carrying Deianira, Hercules' wife, across, he attempted to abduct her and Hercules shot him with a poisoned arrow. The Centaur's revenge, as he lay dying, was to assure Deianira that his blood would restore Hercules' love for her if he should ever stray. When, later, Hercules had ceased to love her she sent him a garment—some accounts have it the actual shirt of Nessus, others state merely a garment stained with the Centaur's blood. It clung to Hercules' body, once he had put it on, and burned his flesh like fire, so that he died in wild agonies.

NESTOR

Nestor

Son of Neleus. He was one of the Argonauts and had taken part in the hunt of the Calydonian Boar. In the *Iliad* he is represented as the grand old man, the sage counselor of the Greeks. But he is garrulous and his counsel is not very specific or effective.

Nibelungenlied

A thirteenth-century German poem which retells, in essence, an early Norse epic known as the VOLSUNG SAGA. In the *Nibelungenlied* Siegfried, son of Siegmund and Sieglind, king and queen of the Netherlands, gets possession of the gold hoard guarded by the dwarf Alberich. He woos Kriemhild, a princess of Burgundy and sister of Gunther. The marriage is agreed upon and the hoard is given to Kriemhild as a marriage gift. Siegfried agrees to help Gunther win Brunhild, queen of Iceland—and the winning consists of defeating her in feats of strength. The two couples are married at the same time. Brunhild is suspicious, Gunther is timid, and Siegfried, impersonating Gunther, subdues Brunhild in the marriage chamber and takes away her ring and girdle, which he gives to Kriemhild—who reveals the humiliating deception to Brunhild. Hagen, a warrior in Gunther's service, feels the honor of his master has been challenged and treacherously kills Siegfried.

Kriemhild marries Etzel (Attila the Hun), at whose court she has her brothers murdered when they refuse to divulge where they have hidden the hoard (they have sunk it in the Rhine). Hagen, the last living person to know where the hoard is, also refuses to tell and is killed by Kriemhild with Siegfried's sword. Kriemhild herself is killed by Hildebrand.

Nibelungs

1. Dwarfs who held the magic hoard.
2. Followers of Siegfried who won the hoard from the dwarfs.
3. The Burgundians under King Gunther.

See NIBELUNGENLIED.

Nidhug (or **Nidhogg**)

A dragon in Norse mythology. It lived in the well HVERGELMIR and gnawed forever at the roots of the life tree YGGDRASIL. At Ragnarok, after Surtr has broken out of Muspellheim and spurted fire over everything, Nidhug will rise from his subterranean depths, to be seen for a moment and then plunge into the bottomless void.

[One feels that Nidhug is echoed in Tennyson's Kraken that sleeps an ancient, dreamless sleep far beneath in the abysmal sea:

> There hath he lain for ages, and will lie
> Battening upon huge sea-worms in his sleep,
> Until the latter fires shall heat the deep;
> Then once by man and angels to be seen,
> In roaring he shall rise and on the surface die.]

Niflheim

In Norse mythology a region of cold, mist, and darkness lying somewhere in the north. In it was Hvergelmir, the great fountain from which flowed ten rivers. And one of the roots of the life-tree Yggdrasil reached into Niflheim and on this root lay the dragon Nidhug, forever gnawing it.

NIGHTINGALE

Nightingale

See AËDON, PHILOMELA.

Nike

The Greek goddess of victory, called *Victoria* by the Romans. She is generally represented as a winged young woman just alighting from flight and carrying a palm branch in one hand, a garland in the other.

Nineve (or Nimue, Nimiane, Vivien)

The Lady of the Lake in Malory's *Morte d'Arthur.* She is a mysterious female of supernatural powers. She gives Arthur the sword Excalibur and when she claims Balin's head is herself killed by Balin. Living again, somehow, she marries Pelleas. When Arthur is sent a jewelled mantle as a gift from Morgan le Fay, Nineve insists that he compel the messenger to put it on first, and when the messenger does so, he bursts into flames and is consumed to ashes. Merlin falls in love with her and she humors him long enough to learn from him a magic spell that permits her to bury him under a huge stone (or, in other versions, to imprison him within an aged oak). She is one of the three queens in the ship which bears the dying Arthur away to Avalon.

[Some scholars insist she is actually Morgan le Fay, which proves how mysterious is (1) Morgan le Fay and (2) Arthurian scholarship.]

Niobe

Daughter of Tantalus and wife of Amphion, king of Thebes. She was the mother of six sons and six daughters (some accounts say seven sons and seven daughters and still others say ten sons and ten daughters) and foolishly boasted that she was better than Leto, who had borne only two children, Apollo and Artemis. But Leto had her two children kill Niobe's many with their invisible arrows. Niobe turned into a fountain with weeping, in some versions of her legend, and into a stone, petrified with grief, in another. She shares with the biblical Rachel ("weeping for her children, and would not be comforted, because they are not") the sad distinction of being the personification of maternal sorrow.

Nisus

King of Megara. He had a lock of purple hair and so long as this lock remained intact upon his head, the city could not fall. But his daughter Scylla fell in love with Minos, who was besieging the city, and she cut off her father's magic lock and brought it to Minos as a gift. But Minos, after capturing the city, rejected her. She was changed into a bird and her father into an eagle which forever pursues her.

Norns

The equivalent in Norse mythology of the Greek Fates. They are three old women, descended from the giants, who feed the roots of YGGDRASIL and mete out men's destinies. They are Urd (the past), Verdandi (the present), and Skuld (the future).

[Their last appearance in literature was as the three Weird Sisters in *Macbeth*.]

Notus

The South Wind.
    See EURUS.

NUMA POMPILIUS

Numa Pompilius

Second king of Rome who, in legend, built the temple of JANUS. It was during his reign that the much-venerated shield of Mars (the *ancile)* fell from the sky.

Nymphs

A class of lesser deities in Greek and Roman mythology. They were conceived of as spirits in the form of young maidens who inhabited woods, trees, and mountains. They often served as attendants upon the major goddesses.

Nyx

The personification in Greek mythology of night—not merely of the daily interval of darkness but of the great darkness that preceded all creation. She is immensely powerful and greatly feared. Zeus himself reverences and consults her and she speaks from her own oracles in stygian caves.

Oceanides

Nymphs of the great ocean stream which, in Greek mythology, flowed continually around the earth.

Oceanus

Son of Uranus and Gaea, husband of Tethys and father of the Oceanides and the river gods. There is very little personal mythology concerning him. He was thought of as a limitless stream that encircles the world—the stream on which, every night in his golden cup, the sun floated around the world in order to regain his starting point in the east.

Ocnus (or **Oknos**)

The personification of incompetence, protracted delay, and confused futility. In Greek lore he is represented as twining a rope of straw which an ass devours as fast as he twines it.

[This sounds vaguely like an oracular foreseeing of a great deal of modern scholarship and graduate study.]

Odin (also **Woden, Wotan, Othin**)

The son of Bor, by the giantess Bestla, he gradually replaced Thor in Norse mythology as the leader of the Aesir. He is the sky god, the All-Father. His wives were Jord and Frigga, and Wednesday is named in his honor. He is the patron of culture, the inventor of runes. He is blind in one eye, having given that eye to drink from Odherir, the magic cauldron or potion of wisdom in the care of the giant Mimir. His other eye is the sun. He will be killed at Ragnarok by the wolf Fenrir.

Odysseus (Latin **Ulysses**)

King of Ithaca. Son of Laertes and Anticlea, husband of Penelope and father of Telemachus. One of the best known of all figures in Greek mythology.

The suitors of Helen solemnly agreed that if anyone took her from whomever she finally chose they would band together to punish her abductor. She chose Menelaus and when Paris (assisted by Aphrodite) carried her off to Troy, Odysseus—one of the suitors—was compelled (*see* PALAMEDES) to keep his word. In the ILIAD he is presented as one of the greatest of the warriors and, at the same time, the most cunning. In post-Homeric literature the unscrupulous and deceitful aspects of his character were stressed, emphasizing his cruelty and treachery. But in Homer he is a noble, if ruthless, figure.

After the ten-year war had finally ended, he commenced his homeward journey to Ithaca and this, the subject of the *Odyssey*, took another ten years, even though the goddess Athena gave him her special protection. Among his many adventures on the way may be mentioned his encounter with the cannibal Laestrygones, the narcotized Lotus-Eaters, the alluring Sirens, the witch Circe, the monster Scylla, the one-eyed giant Polyphemus—and the hero's descent into the underworld and his long sojourn with the nymph Calypso.

Reaching Ithaca at last—though alone, for all of his men were killed in one disaster or another—he found his palace occupied and being despoiled by fifty insolent suitors, who were demanding that his wife, Penelope, marry one of them and who were planning to kill his son Telemachus. Penelope promised to accept one of them when she had finished weaving a shroud for Odysseus' aged father, Laertes, but gained time by secretly unraveling at night what she had woven by day.

Disguised as a beggar and assisted only by two faithful serfs and his as-yet-untried-in-battle son, but possessed again of the mighty bow which he alone can bend, Odysseus slew the suitors (in one of the greatest dramatic passages in all literature) and came at last into his own again.

So ends the *Odyssey*. But in post-Homeric legend Odysseus endures another ten years of wandering and is finally killed by his son by Circe, Telegonus. And, as if *that* weren't enough, Telegonus then marries Penelope and Telemachus marries Circe!

Oedipus

Son of Laius, king of Thebes, and Queen Jocasta (Epicaste in Homer). It was prophesied that the child would kill his father and marry his mother and to thwart this prediction the child's feet were pierced *(Oedipus =* "swollen foot") and it was given to a shepherd who was instructed to let it die of exposure on a mountainside. The shepherd took pity on the child, however, and gave it to another shepherd, who gave it to the childless king and queen of Corinth, Polybus and Merope, who brought it up as their own son.

In his young manhood Oedipus was told by the oracle at Delphi that he would kill his father and marry his mother and, horrified, resolved never to return to what he thought was his native land and his parents. Instead he set out for Thebes and on the way met his real father and (not knowing who he was) killed him in a scuffle over the right-of-way. Approaching Thebes he encountered the Sᴘʜɪɴx and answered the lethal riddle with which she was terrifying the countryside and so compelled the monster to destroy herself. For this he was given the hand of the city's recently widowed queen and so, unwittingly, fulfilled the prophecy. By Jocasta he had four children: Eᴛᴇᴏᴄʟᴇs, Pᴏʟʏɴɪᴄᴇs, Aɴᴛɪɢᴏɴᴇ, and Isᴍᴇɴᴇ. When the facts of the patricide and incest were revealed, Jocasta hanged herself and Oedipus blinded himself and went into exile.

Oeneus

King of Calydon. He was the husband of Althaea and the father of Meleager, Deianira, and Tydeus. He offended Artemis and she sent a savage boar that ravaged his kingdom. A collection of heroes assembled to hunt and slay the boar—which they did—and this became one of the heroic events in Greek mythology. Participation in this hunt was as much, or at least as much-to-be-mentioned, in the credentials of a hero, as to have voyaged with the Argonauts, to have fought at Troy, or to have assaulted or defended Thebes.

Oenomaus

Son of Ares, king of Elis, father of Hippodameia. He demanded of all suitors for his daughter's hand that they engage in a chariot race with him, their lives to be forfeit if they lost. Some versions ascribe this to a prophecy which had told him that he would die when his daughter married and others to his incestuous attachment to the girl. Thirteen suitors had failed and died and Oenomaus had boasted that he would build a pyramid of their skulls. But Pelops, the fourteenth, defeated him by bribing a servant to insert waxen instead of the usual wooden axle pins in Oenomaus' chariot. The wax melted with the heat of the revolving wheels, the wheels came off and Oenomaus was dragged to his death.

Oenone

A nymph on Mount Ida who loved and was beloved by Paris. He deserted her, however, for Helen. She had the power of healing and when he was wounded in the Trojan War he appealed to her to save his life. But, jealous, she refused and he died. Then, overcome by grief and remorse, she killed herself.

[One of Tennyson's finest poems is a lament by Oenone.]

Olympus

A mountain on the border of Macedonia and Thessaly. It is the highest peak in Greece and was considered, in mythology, to be the home of the gods.

Omphale

Queen of Lydia whom Hercules (to expiate a murder committed in madness) served as a slave for three years. In later enlargements of the legend he was made to serve her as a female slave, doing woman's work, while she wore the lion's skin that was the mark of his masculine valor.

Ops

A Roman harvest and fertility goddess. As the wife of Saturn and the mother of Jupiter, she was identified with the Greek Titaness Rhea.

Oracles

The Greeks believed that in many places the gods would give counsel or prophesy the future, sometimes directly but more often through the mediation of an inspired priest who interpreted signs and sounds that to the layman would be meaningless.

The oldest of the oracles was at Dodona and was sacred to Zeus (and/or Hera). Here the oracular utterances were in the form of the rustling of wind in the branches of oak trees or the clashing of metal plates suspended from the swaying branches. Artemis had an oracle at Colchis, Aphrodite at Paphos, Hercules at Athens, Ares in Thrace, Pan in Arcadia, and so on.

The supreme oracle of Greece was that at Delphi, presided over by Apollo, who, at this shrine, was regarded as the mouthpiece of Zeus. It was by far the most sacred of the shrines in Greece. It was supposed to be the center of the earth and was marked by the sacred *omphalos,* the navel-stone (which was also thought to be the stone which, enswaddled, Rhea had given to Cronus to eat when he thought he was devouring the infant Zeus). It had been a holy place from antiquity and the Greeks themselves—in their myth of Apollo's having to kill the Python to take possession—recognized Apollo as a latecomer.

In the functioning of the Delphic oracle, the priestess of the god was seated on a tripod over a fissure in the rock from which, it is thought, may have proceeded hallucinogenic gases or vapors. In reply to the questions of the suppliants the priestess, in a divine ecstasy, uttered incoherent words and these were interpreted by the priests, usually in verses.

Primarily the oracle was concerned with conduct and religion and in such matters it was the supreme authority in Greece. In answers relating to the future the oracle was often equivocal. Thus when the Greeks asked the oracle if they would succeed against the Persians, they were answered that "weeping sires shall tell/ How thousands fought at Salamis and fell." But which side would do more weeping

than the other was not made plain. In fact, in politics the
Delphic oracle discouraged opposing Persia, was pro-Spartan, and supported Philip of Macedon.

The true importance of the Delphic oracle, in the opinion of
many modern scholars, is that it provided a meeting place for
the otherwise so-bitterly-divided Greek city-states.

Orc (or **Ork**)

A devouring monster or ogre. Du Bartas (1598) speaks of an
"Insatiate Orque, that even at one repast/ Almost all creatures in the world would waste." Holland (1650) writes of a
three-headed Orke, but stipulates that this one was "begotten by an incubus."

[The word for the killer whale, Orc, is, apparently from a
different root, though almost as old. Milton *(Paradise Lost,*
XI, 833 ff.) writes of:

> an island salt and bare,
> The haunt of seals and orcs, and sea-mews' clang.]

Orcus

Latin name for Hades, the abode of the dead.

[Milton *(Paradise Lost,* II, 961 ff.) uses the word to designate some ominous and fearful being:

> With him enthroned
> Sat sable-vested Night . . . and by them stood
> Orcus and Ades, and the dreaded name
> Of Demogorgon.]

OREADS

Oreads

Nymphs of mountains and caves.

Orestes

Son of Agamemnon and Clytemnestra, brother of Electra, Iphigenia, and Chrysothemis.

Sent abroad by his mother while his father was away at Troy (that she might enjoy her illicit affair with Aegisthus), he returns after the murder of Agamemnon and kills her and her lover.

The killing of Aegisthus would, in the code of the time, have been regarded as more moral than immoral. But killing his mother, even though she may have merited death and even though he had been commanded to kill her by the great god Apollo, was still matricide, a violation of the fundamental order of nature. And so he was pursued by the EUMENIDES. At a trial before the Areopagus, presided over by Athena, he was purged of his guilt and the Eumenides (in the *Oresteia* of Aeschylus) were persuaded to abandon their persecution.

Orion

A giant, a great hunter who was slain by Artemis and later set in the sky as a constellation. Some accounts say that he was a son of Poseidon and was beloved by Eos, the dawn. One story says that he was blinded by a father whose daughter he was wooing and that he regained his sight by wading through the ocean to the easternmost point, where the rays of the rising sun healed him.

Orpheus

Son of Apollo and Calliope. The greatest of mortal musicians, his playing moved not only beasts of the field but even rocks and inanimate objects. His wife Eurydice was bitten by a snake and died, and her disconsolate husband descended into Hades, where his playing "Drew iron tears down Pluto's cheek,/ And made Hell grant what Love did seek." In the earlier versions his playing gained her complete liberty and they returned to the upper world and happiness. But in later versions Hades stipulated that Orpheus must not look back, on the upward journey, until he was completely clear of the underworld. But the impatience of love was too strong and Orpheus looked back too soon and lost Eurydice forever.

Orpheus died at the hands of a band of Maenads who tore him to pieces and threw his head into the river Hebrus, which carried it to Lesbos ("When, by the rout that made the hideous roar,/ His gory visage down the stream was sent,/ Down the swift Hebrus to the Lesbian shore"). Some versions attribute his death to the fury of the Maenads at his devotion to his dead wife and consequent rejection of them, and others attribute it to Zeus, who had him killed because he placed the worship of Apollo above that of Zeus.

Orthros

The two-headed dog that guarded the red cattle of the monster Geryon. The slaying of Orthros and carrying off of the cattle was Hercules' tenth labor.

Ortygia

The remote island on which the nymph Calypso detained Odysseus for eight years, hoping he would marry her. Zeus sent Hermes to command her to let him go.

Osiris

In Egyptian mythology the god of the dead and ruler of the underworld. Son of earth and sky, husband of his sister Isis, he was killed by his brother Set, the god of evil. He was avenged by his son Horus, who killed Set. Set had cut the dead Osiris into fourteen pieces and scattered these throughout the land. Isis buried them. The gods gave Osiris immortality and made him judge of the underworld. He was depicted as a figure swathed in the wrappings of a mummy.

Ossa (and **Pelion**)

Mountains in Thessaly. The giants OTUS and EPHIALTES trying to scale heaven, planned to pile Ossa upon Olympus and then Pelion on Ossa.

Ossian (properly **Oisin**)

Gaelic warrior and bard, assumed to have lived in the third century A.D. He was the son of Finn (Fingal).

He had an extraordinary revival in the eighteenth century when James Macpherson published (1760–1763), from what he claimed to be original Gaelic documents, a series of bombastic poems presumably written by Ossian. The poems are now generally regarded as a forgery—though certainly one of the most successful and influential literary forgeries ever perpetrated. Chief among those who at the time of the poems' publication challenged their authenticity was Samuel Johnson, who persistently demanded that Macpherson produce the Gaelic manuscripts which he professed to have in his possession. Macpherson blustered but never produced any manuscripts.

[We are grateful to Macpherson if only for being the occasion of one sentence of Johnson's. Macpherson had written an insolent letter to Johnson, threatening to beat him if he did not cease his protests. Johnson answered: "I hope I shall never be deterred from detecting what I think a cheat, by the menaces of a ruffian."]

Otus and Ephialtes

The giant sons of Poseidon and Iphimedeia, wife of Aloeus. They are sometimes called the *Aloadae*. When they were but nine years old they were nine fathoms tall and nine cubits broad and were growing at the rate of nine feet a year. They imprisoned Ares in a bronze jar for thirteen months and he would have perished there had not Eriboia (their step-mother) told Hermes, who thereupon rescued the unhappy god.

They were the juvenile delinquents of Greek theogeny. One account of their death has it that they decided to rape Artemis, the goddess of chastity, and that her brother Apollo drove a deer between them and in shooting at it each killed the other.

Pactolus

A river in Lydia whose sands were changed to gold when MIDAS bathed in it.

Palaemon

A sea divinity in Greek mythology, analogue to the Roman Portumnus, the tutelary deity of ports and shores.

Under the name *Melicertes* he had been the child of INO and ATHAMAS. Ino had nursed Dionysus, one of Zeus' many illegitimate children, and jealous Hera had driven Athamas mad so that he pursued his wife with intent to kill her. Carrying her child, she leaped into the sea, where both of them became minor deities—he thereafter called Palaemon and she Leucothea.

He was usually portrayed riding on a dolphin and was invoked as a savior from shipwreck. The Isthmian Games were celebrated in his honor.

Palamedes

The son of NAUPLIUS. He was an inventor and contests with Cadmus the credit for the invention of the alphabet. He alone among the Greeks compared with Odysseus in cunning and there was animosity between them. When Odysseus tried to get out of his vow to go with the Greeks to Troy, for example, he pretended to be mad and supported the pretense by plowing the sands with a horse yoked to an ox. But at the suggestion of Palamedes, Telemachus, Odysseus' son, then an infant, was placed in the path of the oncoming plow and when Odysseus turned his team aside to avoid killing the child, his trickery was revealed. To be revenged Odysseus hid gold in Palamedes' tent and forged a letter from Priam that indicated that Palamedes had accepted a bribe to betray the Greeks. The ruse worked and Palamedes was put to death.

Pales

The Roman deity of cattle-rearing whose festival, Palilia, was held on April 21.

Palinurus

Aeneas' pilot. Venus begged Neptune to allow her son Aeneas to end his wanderings and reach Italy. Neptune consented but demanded one life as a sort of ritual propitiation. He sent the god Somnus (sleep), who managed to get the helmsman to doze and then pushed him overboard. Palinurus even in his sleep, however, clung to the helm and it came away with him as he went overboard. True to his promise, though, Neptune kept the un-helmed ship on her course until Aeneas himself could take charge. Later, on his way to the underworld, Aeneas saw Palinurus among the wretched ghosts who could not cross the Styx because they had not had due funeral rites. The Sibyl (who was guiding Aeneas) comforted the pilot by assuring him that those who found his body would give it a proper funeral.

PALLADIUM

Palladium

A wooden image of Athena which fell from heaven upon the citadel of Troy and was stolen by Odysseus and Diomedes—since Troy could not be taken while the Palladium remained within its walls. In some accounts it was carried to Greece after the fall of Troy and thence to Rome; in others it was taken directly to Rome by Aeneas. Upon its safe retention depended the welfare and, indeed, the continued existence of the Roman Empire—although, in later times, several cities claimed to have the true Palladium.

[The word *palladium* is used today for anything—but especially something admirable or holy—upon which the safety of a people or a nation is thought to depend.]

Palomydes

A knight in Malory's *Morte d'Arthur* who loves Isolde of Ireland and who defends King Mark of Cornwall in several encounters.

Pan

The god of herds and flocks, of the rustic and pastoral. He had the body of a man but the horns, ears, and legs of a goat. He played on the syrinx and haunted caves and lonely rural places. He was playful, vigorous, and fertile, but irritable, especially if disturbed during his noontime nap. It was dangerous to wake him when he slept in the heat of the afternoon and the shepherds dare not pipe then. He could inspire overwhelming, irrational fears *(panic)* in men and animals. That his name = "all" is "the fancy of theologians" (H. J. Rose).

Plutarch, *On the Cessation of Oracles,* 17, says that in the days of Tiberius, a ship sailing from Greece to Italy was becalmed near the islands of Paxos and Propaxos. Suddenly a voice from the shore three times cried "Tammuz!" And when the pilot (whose name was Tammuz) answered, the voice said, "When you come to Palodes, tell them that great Pan is dead." And when they drifted near Palodes the pilot shouted from the ship "Pan the great is dead" and was answered "by a confused sound of wonderment and great lamentation." On arriving in Italy the pilot was summoned by Tiberius and the scholars attendant upon the emperor decided "it must be the son of Hermes and Penelope, and not the god Pan but a daemon of the same name."

[H. J. Rose thinks they heard the ceremonial lament for Tammuz, or Adonis. The story has a strange ring of reality to it.]

Pandareos

Stole a golden dog, made by Hephaestus, from the temple of Zeus in Crete. In punishment he and his wife were turned into stone and their daughters were carried off by the Harpies.

Pandarus

A Trojan leader who, in the *Iliad* (Book IV), at the instigation of Athena—who hereby hopes to discredit the Trojans—breaks a truce and wounds Menelaus. The Greeks are shocked at this violation of a sacred obligation and Pandarus is killed by Diomedes soon after.

[The modern English use of his name to designate a procurer—a pander—and the act of basely flattering another's vices—derives from Chaucer's representation of Pandar in *Troilus and Criseyde* as the go-between for Troilus and Criseyde. The character was coarsened in Shakespeare's *Troilus and Cressida*.]

PANDORA

Pandora

The first woman. She was Zeus' revenge upon man for having accepted the fire which Prometheus had stolen from heaven. The gods all gave her gifts *(Pandora* = "all gifted") which would make her attractive—and hence dangerous—to man. Epimetheus, Prometheus' brother, despite Prometheus' warning, married her. She had a box or jar in which had been collected all of the world's ills and which she had been told not to open. But her curiosity got the better of her, she opened the box and out flew all the ills that now afflict mankind. Only one remained behind: hope.

Parcae

See FATES.

Paris (also called **Alexander**)

Son of Priam and Hecuba. Serving as a shepherd on Mount Ida, he was called on to judge which of the three goddesses, Hera, Athena, and Aphrodite, was the most beautiful. Bribed by the promise of Helen as his wife, he awarded the golden apple *(see* ERIS) to Aphrodite (Hera having offered the bribe of power and Athena of wisdom). In the Trojan War he fought an inconclusive duel with Menelaus, killed Achilles by shooting him with an arrow in his vulnerable heel, and was himself killed by a poisoned arrow shot by Philoctetes.

Parnassus

A twin-peaked mountain near Delphi. On it are the Corycian cave, sacred to Pan, and the Castalian spring, sacred to Apollo and the Muses. The whole mountain is generally conceived of as sacred to the Muses, especially to the Muse of poetry. One of the twin peaks is sacred to Apollo and the other to Dionysus—suggesting two possible heights of inspiration.

[Our literature is crammed with allusions to Parnassus. Of an aristocratic rimester whose literary pretensions were pandered to by starveling poets, Pope wrote:

> Proud as Apollo on his forked hill,
> Sat full-blown Bufo, puff'd by every quill.
> *(Prol. Satires* 231–32)

One of the best allusions is in Burns' *Epistle to John Lapraik:*

> A set o' dull conceited hashes
> Confuse their brains in college classes!
> They gang in stirks, and come out asses,
>   Plain truth to speak;
> An' syne they think to climb Parnassus
>   By dint o' Greek!]

Pasiphaë

Daughter of Helios, wife of Minos, king of Crete, and mother of Ariadne and Phaedra. Mother of the Minotaur by a bull given to Minos by Poseidon.

See MINOS, DAEDALUS, PHAEDRA.

Patroclus

The dear friend of Achilles. When Achilles sulked in his tent (because Agamemnon had taken from him the maid Briseis), he lent his armor to Patroclus. Mistaking him for Achilles, most of the Trojans fled at his approach, but Hector engaged him in combat and killed him. Achilles, wild with grief and fury, entered the battle and killed HECTOR.

PAX

Pax (or Eirene)

The Roman goddess of peace. In Greek mythology she was one of the HORAE.

Pegasus

The winged horse which, in Greek mythology, sprang from the blood of the decapitated Gorgon, Medusa. The offspring of Poseidon, he was tamed by Athena and presented by her to the Muses. With a stroke of his hoof he caused the fountain Hippocrene to gush forth on Mount Helicon and it became the fountain of the Muses. He is now associated entirely with poetry, but originally bore Zeus' thunderbolt and was for a time the mount of the hero Bellerophon, who captured him with a golden bridle, gift of Athena. With the aid of Pegasus, Bellerophon fought the Chimera, the Amazons, and the Solymi. But when, in overweening pride, Bellerophon tried to ride him up to heaven, Pegasus threw him to his death.

Peisistratus

Nestor's youngest son. In the *Odyssey* he accompanies Telemachus from Pylos to the palace of Menelaus at Sparta.

Peleus

King of the Myrmidons in Thessaly. Father of Achilles by the nymph Thetis. It was at their wedding that Eris, the goddess of discord, threw down the golden apple inscribed "For the fairest," the apple that in time caused the Trojan War.

Pelias

A son of Poseidon. He usurped the throne of his brother Aeson and sent Jason, Aeson's son, to capture the Golden

Fleece, intending the mission to cause the young man's death. But, assisted by Medea, Jason obtained the fleece and returned with it to Iolcus. There Pelias was killed by Medea, who persuaded his daughters to cut him up and boil the pieces, assuring them that this was part of a magic process for restoring their father's youth.

Pelion

See OSSA.

Pellanor (or Pellinore)

A king in the Arthurian legends, father of Sir Lamorak, Sir Percival, and Sir Tor.

Pelleas

An innocent and high-minded young knight in Malory's *Morte d'Arthur.* He is the lover of Ettard (or Ettarre). Pelleas is tricked by Gawain and learns that many of the knights of the Round Table—and even Queen Guinevere—are faithless. After Ettard's death he marries Nineve, the Lady of the Lake.

Pelles

A king in Malory's *Morte d'Arthur* who has the distinction of being closely related "unto Joseph of Arimathie." This, of course, brings him into the GRAIL legends. He is also the father of ELAINE, by whose union with LAUNCELOT he becomes the grandfather of GALAHAD.

Pelopia

Daughter of THYESTES and mother of AEGISTHUS.

Pelops

Son of Tantalus and father of Atreus and Thyestes. When he was a child his father slew him and served him as food to the gods (to test their omniscience). The gods were horrified and indignant, punished Tantalus, and restored Pelops to life —though it was necessary to make him an ivory shoulder, since Demeter, absentminded in her grief for the disappearance of Persephone, ate that part of him. As a young man he wooed and won Hippodameia in a famed chariot race with her homicidal father, OENOMAUS.

See also ATREUS, AGAMEMNON.

Penates

See LARES AND PENATES.

Penelope

Daughter of Icarius of Sparta, wife of Odysseus, and mother of Telemachus. She is best known for her faithfulness to her husband throughout the twenty years of his absence at the Trojan War and in his subsequent wanderings. She was sought in marriage by fifty insolent suitors who insisted that her husband was dead and that she must choose one of them as a second husband. To gain time she said she could not marry until she had finished a web she was weaving—and then secretly unwove at night what she had woven during the day.

See also ODYSSEUS.

Penthesilea

The queen of the Amazons who, after the death of Hector, led her female warriors to the aid of Troy. She fought fiercely but was killed by Achilles—who, after her death, mourned for her so deeply that Thersites accused him of being in love with her. Whereupon Achilles killed Thersites.

Pentheus

King of Thebes. He attempted to stop the worship of Dionysus but was torn to pieces by the wild Maenads in their
orgiastic frenzy—led, by the way, by his own mother, Agave.

Pephredo (= "dread")

One of the GRAIAE.

Percival (or **Perceval, Percyvelle, Parzifal**)

In Malory's *Morte d'Arthur* a son of King Pellanor. He seeks
the Grail and, with Galahad and Bors, is allowed eventually to
see it.

Persephone (Roman **Proserpina**)

Daughter of Zeus and DEMETER. Hades (called also *Dis, Pluto*)
rose suddenly from the underworld and seized her and carried her down to his realm. All growth of vegetation stopped
on the earth while her disconsolate mother—whose Roman
name was Ceres—sought her. Zeus finally ruled that Hades
must give her up unless she had, by some word or act, consented to her own abduction. It turned out that she had eaten
a pomegranate seed (some versions say six pomegranate
seeds) and because of that act she was allowed to return to
the upper world only part of the time. Some accounts state
that she spends six months in the upper world and six
months in the lower world. Others have it three months in
the underworld and nine in the upper world. She is thus at
once a goddess of fertility and a goddess of death and so
matches her spouse Pluto, the god of wealth and the god of
death.

Under the name of *Kore*, Persephone played a large part in
the Eleusinian Mysteries.

PERSEUS

[. . . that fair field
Of Enna, where Proserpin gathering flowers,
Herself a fairer flower, by gloomy Dis
Was gathered—which cost Ceres all that pain
To seek her through the world.
—Milton, *Paradise Lost,* IV, 268 ff.]

Perseus

Son of DANAË, the daughter of Acrisius, king of Argos, by
Zeus. Acrisius had been told by an oracle that his daughter's
son would kill him and to prevent this had imprisoned her in
a tower. But Zeus came to her in the form of a shower of
gold and she bore a son. On learning of the child's birth,
Acrisius set mother and infant afloat in a chest. They drifted
to Seriphus, where they were received by King Polydectes.
Later, when Perseus was a young man, Polydectes (with evil
intent) sent him to fetch the head of the Gorgon Medusa. By
the help of Athena, who gave him a magic sword, winged
sandals, the helmet of invisibility, and a mirror in which he
could safely view the monster, he succeeded in this task. On
his way back he rescued and married ANDROMEDA and on
reaching Seriphus exposed the head of Medusa and turned
Polydectes to stone. He returned the sword, sandals, and
magic helmet to Athena and gave her the head of Medusa.
Later he went to Argos to visit his grandfather, Acrisius, and,
in the course of some games, accidentally struck him with a
discus and killed him, thus fulfilling the prophecy.

Phaeacians

The peace-loving, luxurious, hospitable people who—under
their king Alcinous and his queen Arete—received the shipwrecked Odysseus with kindness, heard his story, and offered him the hand of their princess, Nausicaa. But when he

declined the proffered honor, they felt no resentment but loaded him with treasure and had him conveyed to Ithaca in one of their magic ships, ships that needed no pilots. Their women surpassed all other women in weaving and the domestic arts and their men surpassed all other men in navigation. They prided themselves on helping shipwrecked men. But the god Poseidon resented this, as an implied slight to his power, and turned the ship that had carried Odysseus safely to Ithaca into a rock.

Phaedra

See HIPPOLYTUS.

Phaëthon

The son of the sun god Helios. He asked his father to let him drive the chariot of the sun for one day, but he was unable to control the powerful horses and the chariot plunged madly towards earth, searing that part of the earth we call the Sahara. And all would have been destroyed had not Zeus struck the hapless youth with a thunderbolt.

Phaon

A ferryman, ferrying between Lesbos and Chios, who good-naturedly gave Aphrodite, disguised as an ugly old woman, a free passage on his boat. In return she gave him a magic salve which made him young and irresistibly beautiful. The women of Lesbos all fell in love with him and the poetess Sappho is said to have thrown herself into the sea because he did not requite her affection.

[This represents Sappho as having a wider range of interest than is commonly attributed to her.]

PHEMIUS

Phemius

The bard in Odysseus' palace who begs Odysseus to spare his life, insisting that he had sung for the suitors only under duress. Telemachus intercedes for him and Odysseus spares him.

Philemon

When Zeus and Hermes came to earth disguised, on one occasion, to test human kindness, they were refused food and lodging by all but a simple, devoted old rustic couple, Philemon and his wife Baucis. There are various accounts of the rewards given to them. One is that they were given an inexhaustible pitcher. Another that they were forewarned of a flood that destroyed the other inhabitants of their land. But the best known (from Ovid) is that when asked what they most desired they replied that they would like to die at the same time. The wish was granted and they were changed into trees.

Philoctetes

Son of Poias, from whom he had inherited Hercules' invincible bow and mortal arrows. He joined the Greeks against the Trojans. But on the way to Troy he had been bitten by a serpent and the wound had smelled so offensively and its pain had caused Philoctetes to cry out so continuously that the Greeks had marooned him on the island of Lemnos. The captured Trojan seer Helenus had told the Greeks, however, that they could not hope to win Troy without the bow and arrows of Hercules. And so Odysseus and Diomedes (in some accounts Neoptolemus) had gone to Lemnos and had persuaded the bitterly resentful Philoctetes to rejoin them, and the sons of Aesculapius—Machaon and Podalerius—had cured the wound. Philoctetes slew Paris with one of his arrows and helped to win the final victory.

[Edmund Wilson, in a series of critical essays collected under the title *The Wound and the Bow* used Philoctetes—with his incurable wound and his invincible bow—as a type or symbol of the creative artist.]

Philoetius

Odysseus' chief cowherd. He remained faithful to his master and stood by him in the battle with the suitors.

Philamela

Daughter of Pandion, king of Athens, and sister of Procne. Procne was wife to Tereus, king of Thrace. Tereus wrote to Pandion saying that Procne was dead and asking that Philomela be sent to him. On her arrival he raped her and then cut out her tongue so that she could not inform against him. However she managed to communicate the facts to her sister by means of a piece of embroidery and Procne avenged her sister by killing the child Itys (or Itylus), which she had borne to Tereus, and serving him up to his father in a meal. The women fled and Tereus pursued them. But the gods intervened and changed him to a hoopoe, Procne to a nightingale, and Philomela to a swallow.

In another version, it was Procne who had her tongue cut out.

Phineus

Aged blind king of Salmydessus. There are various stories to account for his blindness. One is that he foolishly revealed certain divine secrets into possession of which he had come by means of prophetic powers he had.

Another story says that he allowed his second wife to blind

the children of his first wife. Zeus, shocked at this inhumanity, gave him his choice of death or blindness. He chose blindness and this offended Helios, who sent the Harpies—foul, bird-like creatures that snatched his food from the table and so befouled it that he could not eat it. He was freed from them by the sons of Boreas, who accompanied the Argonauts, in return for his promise to use his powers of prophecy in the Argonauts' behalf.

Phlegethon

The river of fire, one of the five rivers of the underworld in Greek mythology. It flowed into Acheron, the river of woe.

Phoebe (= "the shining one")

A Titaness, daughter of Uranus and Gaea, wife of Coeus and mother of LETO.

Phoebus (= "shining")

Another name for Apollo. It stresses his brightness as the sun god and is often used in conjunction with his name—as Phoebus Apollo.

[The names of Latin deities were much affected by the nineteenth-century upper-class British as genteel profanity. The Elizabethans, forbidden to use the word *God* on the stage, had mocked the edict with blasphemous impudence and substituted *cod*. But the nineteenth-century public-school aristocrat preferred snobbery to wit and sought pseudo-Olympian solace in "By Jove" and "By Jupiter." *Phoebus* ("Amos Cottle!—Phoebus! what a name"—Byron) had the advantage of at least echoing the vowels and syllabification of *Jesus!*]

Phoenix

The Greek name for the Egyptian mythological bird, *Bennu,* a symbol for the rising sun. The bird, the only one of its kind, lived for five hundred years at a time, somewhere in the Arabian wilderness. At the end of that time it built its own funeral pyre of gums and spices, lighted the pyre with the beating of its wings, and was consumed to ashes. Out of the ashes grew a new Phoenix which, in time, repeated the process. In medieval Christian writings it was a symbol of the Resurrection of Jesus Christ.

Phorcys

A sea god, begetter of various horrors and monsters. On his sister Ceto he begot the GRAIAE, the GORGONS, and the dragon Ladon that guarded the Golden Apples of the Hesperides. On HECATE he begot the monster SCYLLA.

Phrixus and Helle

Son and daughter of ATHAMAS by Nephele, who, to save them from persecution by Ino, Athamas' second wife, sent them to Colchis on the back of a flying, golden-fleeced ram. Crossing from Europe to Asia, Helle fell off into the sea (thereafter named the *Hellespont).* But Phrixus reached Colchis and sacrificed the ram. He was, however, murdered by King Aeëtes, who coveted the creature's golden fleece.

Phyleus

The son of Augeas who, when his father refused to give Hercules the reward he had promised him for cleaning the stables *(see* AUGEAN STABLES), testified against his father and was banished.

PHYLLIS

Phyllis

See DEMOPHON.

Picus

A Roman deity, son of Saturn, father of Faunus, and the husband of either Canens or Pomona. Circe loved him and when he rejected her she changed him to a woodpecker.

A god of agriculture, he is particularly the god of manure.

Pillars of Hercules

The tenth of Hercules' fabled labors was to capture the oxen of the three-bodied monster Geryon, who lived on Erythea, an island in the far west. Reaching the western extremities of Europe and Africa, Hercules, in one account, raised the two mountains of Abyla and Calpe—which were thereafter the Pillars of Hercules. In another account he split a mountain in two and left one-half on each side of what is now the Strait of Gibraltar.

Pirithous

One of the Lapithae. Son of Zeus and friend of Theseus. At his wedding to Hippodameia, the Centaurs, who had been invited, attempted to abduct the bride and a great fight ensued in which the Centaurs were defeated. In another story, Pirithous accompanied Theseus on a foray into the underworld to carry off Persephone. They did not succeed. Theseus, however, managed to escape but Pirithous did not.

Pleiads (or Pleiades)

Seven nymphs, daughters of Atlas and attendants in Artemis' train. They were pursued by the giant Orion, and Zeus, to effect their escape, changed them into a constellation. But in the constellation only six of them are even faintly visible. Of the invisible seventh there are two accounts:

(1) that she is Electra, who left her place with her sisters because she could not bear to see the destruction of Troy, which was founded by her son Dardanus. (In this account, it was the spectacle of that fall that caused the remaining six to become so pale);
(2) that she is Merope, who lost her immortality by marrying Sisyphus, king of Corinth.

Pluto

One of the names of Hades, god of the underworld. It is connected with PLUTUS.

Plutus

A personification of wealth, especially the wealth of crops. Hence often represented as a son of Demeter and associated with her in the Eleusinian Mysteries. Since he came out of the ground (as also does mineral wealth), he was also associated with Hades, who frequently was called Pluto.

Pollux

See CASTOR AND POLLUX.

Polydamas

"Prudent Polydamas" who gave his fellow Trojans "excellent counsel" in the eighteenth book of the *Iliad,* urging them to retreat behind the safety of Troy's walls and not to encounter the wrath of Achilles on the open plain. Hector "scowlfully eyeing him" rebuked him for this suggestion and the other Trojans shouted approval of Hector's rebuke, "for Pallas Athena bereft them of wisdom."

POLYDORUS

Polydorus

1. Youngest son of Priam and Hecuba. Priam sent him with gold to POLYMESTOR and he was murdered for the gold.
2. One of the EPIGONI.

Polyeidus

A seer. Minos of Crete commanded him to restore his dead son, Glaucus, to life, the child having died from falling into a vat of honey. Polyeidus saw a snake approaching the dead child and killed the snake. Another snake appeared and seeing its mate dead went away and returned with an herb which restored the dead snake to life. Polyeidus used the same herb on the dead child and brought it back to life.

Polyhymnia

The Muse of sacred song.

Polymestor

Son-in-law of Priam and king of the Thracian Chersonese. To him, for safe-keeping, Priam and Hecuba sent their young son Polydorus and with him a treasure to defray the costs of his care and education. Polymestor murdered the boy for the gold and Hecuba, finding the child's body washed up on the shore, sent word to Polymestor that she could show him a treasure concealed in the ruins of Troy. When his greed led him to put himself into her power, she murdered his two sons and tore out his eyes. There are several versions of the story, all equally gruesome.

Polynices

See ETEOCLES.

POSEIDON

Polyphemus

1. Son of Elatus, the Arcadian, one of the Argonauts.
2. Son of Poseidon, one of the CYCLOPS. Odysseus blinded him in order to escape from his cave, wherein he was holding Odysseus and his men prisoners that he might devour them at his leisure.

Polyxena

Daughter of Priam, beloved by Achilles (who had seen her during the truce which was allowed the Trojans for the burial of Hector). After Achilles' death his ghost demanded her in marriage and when Troy fell she was sacrificed on his tomb.

Pomona

The Roman goddess of fruit trees.

Pontus

A personification of the sea.

Poseidon (Roman **Neptune**)

Son of Cronus and Rhea, hence full brother of Zeus and Hades. Originally a god of earthquakes and water, he became the supreme god of the sea and, as such, is represented as tempestuous, subject to sudden and violent rages, vindictive. He is rarely mild or peaceful. His consort is Amphitrite. He bears a trident as his symbol and is accompanied by Nereids, Tritons, and sea monsters of all kinds. He is the father of many of these monsters. He begets giants, such as Orion and Polyphemus. He sired the winged horse Pegasus upon the Gorgon Medusa. One of the commonest of the Homeric epithets for the sea is "unharvested"; it was barren, non-human.

He is the god of horses—perhaps from the suggestion of

the manes of galloping horses in breaking waves. Upon Demeter he begot the speaking horse Arion.

In the *Odyssey* he is represented as the implacable foe of Odysseus, who had blinded his son Polyphemus.

Priam

King of Troy at the time of its siege and destruction by the Greeks. He is the father of fifty sons, nineteen of whom proceeded from the "o'er teemed loins" of his queen Hecuba. Other queens and concubines produced the remaining thirty-one. Many versions said there were fifty daughters as well, though only two of these, CASSANDRA and POLYXENA have received much mention.

Priam is represented in the *Iliad* as a gentle, revered old man. When the greatest of his sons, Hector, is slain by Achilles, Priam goes to Achilles to beg his son's body and by his grief moves Achilles to pity. At the sack of Troy he is killed by Neoptolemus (Pyrrhus), Achilles' son.

Priapus

Son of Dionysus and Aphrodite. The god of fertility and generation, especially in its coarser aspects.

Procne

See PHILOMELA.

Procrustes (also called **Damastes, Polypemon**)

A giant robber, son of Poseidon. He is known chiefly for a famous, or infamous, bed which he offered, in the guise of hospitality, to his victims. If they were too short for the bed, he stretched their limbs until they fit. If they were too long for the bed, he lopped off however much was necessary to make them fit. Theseus killed him by shortening him to fit his own bed.

[Hence our adjective *procrustean:* "tending to produce conformity by violent means."]

Prometheus

Son of Iapetus and the ocean nymph Clymene. In many legends he is represented as a friend to mankind. Thus when Zeus denied fire to men, Prometheus stole it from heaven and gave it to man. By means of a trick Prometheus arranged for men to get the best meat in sacrifices, giving the gods the poorer parts wrapped in fat. He tried to prevent man from accepting Zeus' deceptive gift of woman *(see* PANDORA).

In the best known of the myths that have gathered around Prometheus he is forever chained to a rock in the Caucasus where a vulture or an eagle tears out his liver. In some accounts this is his punishment for the trickery in regard to the sacrifices. In others it is having stolen the fire. But (in later writers, beginning with Aeschylus) the thing is far more dramatic: Prometheus knows that if Zeus has a child by the nymph Thetis, their son will be mightier than Zeus and will destroy him. And he accepts the torture on the rock rather than reveal this secret, since his *not* revealing it gives him power over Zeus. In some accounts he is persuaded to reveal the secret and is freed by Hercules. In others (which particularly appealed to such romantics as Shelley), he remains the personification of the unconquerable will opposing tyranny, forever chained and suffering but confident of the ultimate triumph of his cause.

Proserpina

Roman form of the Greek PERSEPHONE.

PROTESILAUS

Protesilaus

A prophecy having foretold that the first man from the Greek fleet to set foot on the shore at Troy would be killed, Protesilaus deliberately leaped ashore, offering himself as a patriotic sacrifice, and was slain.

See also LAODAMIA.

Proteus

A sea god who had the power to assume many shapes. He was a seer and if a questioner could hold on to him throughout his transformations, he would answer the question put to him. Menelaus, in the *Odyssey,* compels him to tell him how to get back to Sparta. Proteus was a seal herder and an added difficulty the pertinacious questioner had to endure was "the deathly stench of the sea-born seals." He is known as the Ancient One of the Sea or the Old Man of the Sea.

Psyche

A mortal maiden beloved by Eros. Or, more properly, by Cupid, since the story first appeared in a Latin work of the second century A.D., *The Golden Ass* of Lucius Apuleius. Cupid conveyed her to a lonely place where every night he came to her but remained invisible. He ordered her not to attempt to see him and when, overcome by love and curiosity, she violated his command, he left her. She wandered about the world seeking him, enduring many hardships, until at last Jupiter made her immortal and the lovers were reunited.

Ptah

The chief of the Egyptian gods. He was represented in human form, always holding the *ankh,* the symbol of life and the generative, creative forces. He was in some aspects a smith god and was sometimes identified by the Greeks with Hephaestus.

Pygmalion

1. King of Cyprus who fashioned the statue of a woman and fell in love with his own creation. Aphrodite gave the statue life, Pygmalion married her, and they had a daughter, Paphos. The statue-woman was not called Galatea until much later.

[G. B. Shaw's *Pygmalion* was the basis of the popular musical show *My Fair Lady*.]

2. Brother of Dido, queen of Carthage.

Pylades

Son of Strophius. The friend and attendant of ORESTES.

Pyramus and Thisbe

Not strictly mythology, the story of Pyramus and Thisbe is simply an old love story that first appeared in Ovid's *Metamorphoses*—almost literally in the year One. They were young lovers in Babylon. Forbidden by their parents to meet, they talked through a crack in a wall. They finally arranged to meet at a tomb outside the city. Thisbe arrived first, was terrified by a lion and fled, dropping her veil, which the lion nuzzled. Pyramus arrived to find the blood-stained veil and, assuming she had been killed by the lion, killed himself. She returned, found him dead, and killed herself.

Pyrrha

See DEUCALION.

PYRRHIC VICTORY

Pyrrhic Victory

A victory gained at too great a cost. Pyrrhus, king of Epirus, defeated the Romans at Asculum and Apulia in 279 B.C. But he achieved victory only at the cost of cripplingly severe losses. Congratulated on the victory, Pyrrhus replied, "Another such victory and we are ruined."

Pyrrhus

1. *See* NEOPTOLEMUS.
2. *See* PYRRHIC VICTORY.

Python

A female dragon born from the mud of Deucalion's flood. The oracle at Delphi was at first her oracle and it was only by slaying her that Apollo made the shrine—the most sacred in all Greece—his. The actual seat of the inspired priestess at Delphi was called the *Pythia*.

Queen Quinevere

See GUINEVERE.

Queen Morgan le Fay

See MORGAN LE FAY.

Quirinus

A Roman god of war whose name commonly was associated in a triad with Jupiter and Mars. He was thought to be a deification of Romulus.

Ra

The sun god, one of the supreme Egyptian deities. He is sometimes represented with a falcon head but more often as a bearded man crowned with the solar disk. His symbols were the falcon and the scarab, or dung beetle.

Ragnarok

The great final battle, in Norse mythology, between the gods and the giants, in which all shall be destroyed except seven of the Aesir (Balder, Hoder, Hoenir, Magni, Modi, Vali, and Vidar).

For imaginative violence few passages in literature or folklore can equal it. Heimdal will blow the full blast on the Gjaller Horn. The heroes will rush out of Valhalla. Odin will be swallowed by the Fenris-wolf, and avenged by his son Vidar. Thor will slay the Midgard Serpent, only to drown in its venom. Tyr and Garm will kill each other. As also will Loki and Heimdal. Two Jotuns will swallow the sun and the moon. Yggdrasil will crack and crumble. Nidhug will rise from Hvergelmir only to plunge into the void of Ginnungagap. Etc., etc. All of the violence that has ever occurred on the earth will be but a fleabite to it.

Ran

Sea goddess, sister and wife of Aegir (Gymir), who is the equivalent in Norse mythology of Poseidon or Neptune. Ran, however, reflects the cruel cold of the North Sea rather than the sunlit Mediterranean: she is greedy and drags down the drowning.

Regin

The blacksmith who educated Sigurd the Volsung and forged for him his matchless sword *Gram*. Regin was brother to FAFNIR and egged Sigurd on to kill Fafnir. This Sigurd did but having learned the language of birds (from eating Fafnir's heart) he learned that Regin was planning treachery against him and so slew Regin as well.

Remus

See ROMULUS.

Rhadamanthus

One of the three stern judges of the underworld. He was a son of Zeus and Europa, as was another of the judges, Minos. The third, King Aeacus, was the son of Zeus and Aegina.

Rhea

The sister and wife of CRONUS. She was identified by the Romans with OPS and later, as Cybele ("the Mighty Mother"), was worshipped widely in Asia Minor. Her worship as Cybele involved frenzied excesses led and stimulated by her priests, the Corybantes.

RHESUS

Rhesus

King of Thrace, an ally of the Trojans in the Trojan War. It was foretold that if he or his horses drank the waters of the Scamander (a river that flowed by Troy), Troy would be invulnerable. Therefore, the very day he arrived, before he or his horses could drink, Odysseus and Diomedes stole into his camp and killed him and carried off the horses.

[The Rhesus monkey is named after the short-lived hero, but arbitrarily, for no reason of resemblance or any other connection. The creature was so named in 1839, when everyone who had had any education at all had had a classical education, and the selection of this name may have been some humorous zoologist's reflection on the utter irrelevance of that education to his scientific pursuits.]

Rhoecus

By propping up a falling oak tree, Rhoecus saved the life of its HAMADRYAD. He fell in love with her and she reciprocated his love. He was to return at a certain time and to communicate with her, while apart from her, by her messenger, a bee. But he became engrossed in gambling and injured the bee, brushing it aside. When he remembered the tryst and ran madly to it, it was too late and the nymph deprived him of his sight.

[James Russell Lowell wrote a poetic version of this myth.]

Rinda

A giantess, wife of Odin in Norse mythology.

Romulus and Remus

Sons of Mars and a Vestal Virgin, Rhea Silvia. The infants were set adrift in a small vessel in the flooded Tiber, but it was washed ashore and they were rescued and suckled by a she-wolf. Grown to man's estate, they founded the city of Rome. Romulus built the walls of the city and killed Remus for showing his contempt by jumping over them. After ruling for forty years Romulus vanished and became the god Quirinus.

Round Table

The famous Round Table was made by the wizard Merlin for Uther Pendragon. He gave it to King Laudegreaunce (or Leodegraunce), who gave it as a wedding present to King Arthur when he married Guinevere, Laudegreaunce's daughter. Much importance was formerly attached to one's place at table in relation to the head, especially as to whether one were seated above or below the salt. So the circularity of the Round Table indicated the equality of those seated at it. It seated 150 or, rather, 151, for one place (the "Siege Perilous") was always left vacant, waiting for that knight who should find the Holy GRAIL.

[A number of circular tables, some very old, have been claimed to be the authentic Round Table. Others were built in emulation. King Edward III (1312–1377) is said to have had one constructed that was two hundred feet in diameter. One of the Round Tables, at least so called, now hangs in the castle at Winchester. Professor Arthur W. Brown, of Northwestern University, devoted a long and learned life to proving that the Round Table may have been square.]

Rungnir

A brawling Jotun who challenged Thor to a duel. Thor killed the giant but as he fell one of his legs lay across Thor and none of the gods were able to lift it. However, they bethought themselves to send in haste for Magni, Thor's infant son, who was strong enough to lift the dead giant's leg and free his father.

Ryence (or Ryons, Royns)

A Welsh king in Malory's *Morte d'Arthur* who sent an insolent message to King Arthur demanding his beard wherewith to finish trimming his mantle, having already adorned it with the beards of eleven other kings. He was taken prisoner by Balin and Balan.

Saehrimnir

A boar which was daily cooked and eaten by the heroes in Valhalla but was magically replenished the next day.

Salacia

In Roman mythology the wife of Neptune and hence the goddess of the sea—in contrast to various minor deities that presided over streams, lakes, springs, and so on.

Salmoneus

King of Elis. He appears in the *Aeneid* as an eccentric or madman who pretended to be Zeus, flung torches around to simulate the thunderbolts and rejoiced in the thunderous rumbling of his chariot. Zeus—not a patient god nor one whose fancy was tickled by human whimsies—hit the luckless Salmoneus with a real thunderbolt.

Salus

The Roman goddess of health and public well-being.

Sarpedon

Son of Zeus and Europa, he was a Lycian hero who fought on the Trojan side in the Trojan War and was killed by Patroclus.

SATURN

In some accounts he is said to have lived for three generations.

Saturn

An old Italian king-god, a harvest god, who came to be equated with the Greek Cronus. He begot the major gods and in his reign was the Golden Age. His wife was Ops, the goddess of fruitfulness.

The planet Saturn is named after him, as also is Saturday. Our *saturnalia* derives from the Roman festival held, in December, in his honor. It was marked by revelry and merrymaking and in its course slaves were served by their masters to commemorate the fact that in the Golden Age there had been no social distinctions.

Satyrs

Forest gods, usually attendant upon Dionysus. Like the fauns and Pan (Faunus) they had the head, arms, and torso of a man but had a goat's ears, small horns, and the hindquarters of a goat. They are represented as dancing, playing upon reed pipes and, above all, chasing nymphs, for they were very lecherous.

See also PAN, SILENUS.

Scamander

A small river that flows into the Hellespont near Troy. Its waters were thought to be especially beautifying and Hera, Athena, and Aphrodite all bathed in it and, in particular, rinsed their hair in it, before they entered the fateful beauty contest on Mount Ida. In one of those unexpected little human touches that contribute to the forcefulness of the great epics, we are told in the *Iliad* that Hector's affectionate name for his infant son, Astyanax, was Scamandrius.

Scylla

1. Daughter of Phorcys and Ceto (or, in some accounts, Hecate). She was a six-headed sea monster, and each of her six heads had three rows of teeth. Her lower limbs were snakes and barking dogs. She was immortal and invincible and lived in a cave opposite Charybdis—and a nice illustration of the range of Greek imagination is given in the fact that Circe warned Odysseus that, of the two, he *must* take his chances with Scylla! As he did, thereby, to his grief, losing six men. Some legends state that she was once human and was changed to her fearful state by either Circe or jealous Amphitrite.

2. Daughter of Nisus, king of Megara.

Sekhmet

Lion-headed Egyptian fire goddess, the wife of Ptah and the mother of Imhotep. Her sister Bast was a cat-headed fire goddess.

Selene

The Greek goddess of the moon. In many ways she corresponded to the Roman Diana, but there were significant differences. Diana, for instance, was a huntress; Selene was not. Diana was a virgin; Selene had fifty daughters by Endymion and several others by Zeus.

Semele

See Dionysus.

Semiramis

In Babylonian mythology the queen (practically for a day) of Ninus, the founder of Nineveh. She persuaded him to make her queen for five days and in that five days had him killed, then took over the government and built Babylon, conquered Persia and Egypt, etc. She was sometimes identified with the fertility goddess Ishtar.

Serapis

The sacred dead Apis bull in Egyptian mythology. In him Osiris (and sometimes Ptah) was believed to be incarnate. He was ruler of the underworld and in Greece was identified with Hades.

Set

The Egyptian god of darkness and evil. He is the brother and killer of Osiris. In Greek mythology he was identified with TYPHON.

Setebos

A god presumably worshipped by the Patagonians, mentioned by Magellan and Sir Francis Drake and alluded to by Shakespeare in *The Tempest* as the god of Sycorax, Caliban's mother. Browning has a monologue in which Caliban meditates upon the nature of this god—*Caliban upon Setebos.*

Seven Against Thebes

Eteocles and Polynices, sons of OEDIPUS, agreed, after his exile, to rule the city, each by alternate years. Eteocles, the elder of the two, ruled the first years but at the expiration he refused to relinquish his power and exiled his brother.

Polynices gathered six friends and their armies to march on Thebes. An oracle having stated that victory would fall to whichever side had Oedipus with them, both sons attempted to persuade or force their father to join with them. But all their pleas received was an embittered curse.

Each of the Seven took up a position before one of the city's seven gates. Great feats of valor were done, but the city could not be taken, since Menoeceus, the son of CREON 1, had obtained the goodwill of the gods by offering himself as a sacrifice to save his native city.

The Seven were: Adrastus, Amphiaraus, Capaneus, Eteocles (son of Hipponous), Parthenopaeus, Polynices, and Tydeus. Capaneus boasted that he would force his way into Thebes despite the opposition of Zeus—and was killed by a thunderbolt. Amphiaraus was swallowed into a chasm opened in the earth by another thunderbolt. Polynices was killed in single combat with his brother, each slaying the other. Only Adrastus survived of all the Seven.

See also OEDIPUS, ANTIGONE, ADRASTUS, AMPHIARAUS, POLYNICES.

Sibyl(s)

A Sibyl was a prophetess, usually conceived of as a very old woman. There are a number of Sibyls, perhaps a dozen in all: the Erythraean, the Phrygian, the Samian, the Delphic, and so on.

Of these Amalthea, the Cumaean Sibyl, who assisted Aeneas in his journey into the underworld, is the best known. And of her there are two particular legends. The first is that she was loved by Apollo and asked him for as many years of life as she could hold grains of sand in her cupped hands. Her request was granted, but she had forgotten to ask for eternal youth and so grew inconceivably old and withered. The other is that she offered to sell Tarquin nine volumes of the Sibylline Books, and when her offer was declined she burned three of them and then offered him the remaining six at the price of the original nine. And when that was declined, she burned three more and offered him the remaining three at the price first asked for the nine. And this offer was hastily accepted.

Siegfried

Hero of the first part of the *Nibelungenlied*—the story of the NIBELUNGS. Like ACHILLES, Siegfried was invulnerable in all but one place on his body. In Siegfried this was a spot between the shoulder blades on which a leaf had fallen as he was bathing in the blood of the dragon Fafnir, which he had slain.

He married KRIEMHILD and carried off BRUNHILD for GUN-THER, his brother-in-law. But Gunther was jealous—probably with good reason—and Brunhild (having discovered the secret spot of Siegfried's vulnerability) had him murdered by Hagen. Some versions state that it was at her urging, others that Hagen acted on his own impulse.

Sif

Thor's second wife. She was the mother of Ull, who was the champion skier among the Norse gods. Loki stole Sif's blonde hair and was forced to replace it with hair made of pure gold by the dwarfs.

Siggeir

King of Gothland who seized the kingdom of the Volsungs. He killed Volsung and had a she-wolf devour nine of his sons. Only Sigmund escaped and later, with the help of his son Sinfiotli, he killed Siggeir's children and burned Siggeir.

Sigurd

Hero of the VOLSUNG SAGA.

Silenus and **Sileni**

A bearded, shaggy old man, usually drunk and riding on an ass, attendant upon Dionysus, to whom he was a sort of foster father. The individual god came later in Greek mythology than the group of which he was a representative or type, there having been many sileni. Silenus (and the sileni) was thought to be very wise, even though debauched and, like the satyrs with whom he was associated, lascivious. It is said that King Midas learned great wisdom from Silenus, but what it was nobody ever knew because—like the wisdom which Thomas Hardy professed to have learned at the end of his life—except for the fact that it is better not to be born, it was too dreadful to be spoken.

Silvanus

An old Italian god, related to Pan and Faunus. He watched over herdsmen and boundaries, over plowmen and woodcutters, forests and plowed fields. Like Pan he was generally friendly but had the power to instill sudden, unreasonable fear.

Either much earlier than this, or in some later development, he was thought of as something dangerous that must be propitiated. At the birth of a child the Romans had a custom of pounding, sweeping, and chopping "to keep off Silvanus." These noises of domesticity may have been an assertion against the resentful god of the undomesticated.

SILVIUS

Silvius

Son of Aeneas and Lavinia.

Sinfiotli

Son of Sigmund and his sister Signy in the VOLSUNG SAGA.

Sinon

Son of Sisyphus. It was he who persuaded the Trojans to breach their walls and take in the fatal TROJAN HORSE. For this he became a name for treachery, often mentioned in the same rhetorical breath with Judas Iscariot and with Genilon, who betrayed Roland at the Pass of Roncesvalles, persuading Charlemagne that the trumpet blast calling for help was merely a hunting cry.

[So Chaucer, in *The Nun's Priest's Tale* of the "col-fox, ful of sly iniquitee" that lay in wait for the unsuspecting Chanticleer:

> O false mordrour, lurkynge in thy den!
> O newe Scariot, newe Genylon,
> False dissymulour, O Greek Synon,
> That broughtest Troye al outrely to sorwe!]

Sirens

Half-women, half-birds, they lived on an island near Scylla and Charybdis and by their melodious song lured men to their death. The Argonauts heard them and would have perished had not Orpheus, who accompanied them, played even more enchantingly than the Sirens sang. Odysseus heard them and survived because he had his men fill their ears with beeswax (so they could not hear) and then tie him to the mast (so that he could hear but could not jump overboard).

The Sirens were doomed to die when mortals could listen to them and yet resist them, and after these two defeats they leaped into the sea and were changed to rocks. In the *Odyssey* there were two of them, but in later representations there were three. Their names were Parthenope, Leucosia, and Ligeia.

For some reason the nature of the Sirens' song was, for centuries, a byword for the utterly unknown. The emperor Tiberius, who prided himself on his minute knowledge of mythology, used to taunt the grammarians at his court by demanding of them "What was the song the Sirens sang?" But in the *Odyssey* it is stated that the "honey-sweet music of their lips" was the promise of knowledge.

[One of the Argonauts, Butes, was either tone deaf or highly susceptible to alluring females. Despite Orpheus' playing he leaped overboard but, fortunately, was saved by Aphrodite. The significance is puzzling. Does it mean that he found the fishy ladies, on closer approach, anaphrodisiac? Or that love and learning don't go together?]

Sisyphus

Son of Aeolus. Best known today for being required throughout eternity to roll a huge stone to the top of a hill only to have it plunge back down just as it reaches the crest. Hence a symbol of futility.

But in Greek mythology he was more famed for his trickery and was, indeed, a comic rogue-hero. Thus he stopped Autolycus (a rival rogue) from stealing his cattle—after several depredations—by attaching to the animals' hooves lead plates that imprinted "stolen by Autolycus" in the dust and mud as they were driven away.

Various accounts attribute his punishment of rolling the great stone uphill to various crimes. But there is also a humorous explanation. When Thanatos (death) came for him, Sisyphus bound him and hence no one died until Zeus intervened. Sisyphus himself was then taken to Hades but managed to get a temporary leave in order to go back and punish his wife for not giving him a proper burial—though, actually, he had ordered her not to give him a proper burial, but to throw his body in the street, so that he would have an excuse for returning. Once out of the underworld, however, he wouldn't return and, by various shifts, stayed away until he died of old age. In this story he was set his eternal task as a means of keeping him too busy to plan another escape.

Skade

Daughter of the storm Jotun Tjasse. She demanded payment from the Aesir for her father's death. They let her choose one of the gods for her husband and thus become a goddess. But she had to make her choice from seeing the gods' legs only. She chose Njord. She was the goddess of skiers.

Skidbladnir

In Norse mythology, a ship made for Frey by the dwarfs. It served equally well in the air and on the water. It was large enough to hold all the gods, their horses, and their gear, and yet it could be folded up and carried in a pocket.

Skrymir

King of the Frost Giants in Norse mythology. Under the name of Utgard-Loki (= "outermost-dwelling wicked magician") he once entertained Thor, Thjalfi, and Loki. The visiting gods, unaware of their host's identity, were challenged to a series of competitions, in all of which, to their chagrin, they were worsted. Loki was defeated in eating, Thjalfi in running, and Thor in drinking, in attempting to lift a cat, and in wrestling with an old woman. But, it turned out, Loki's opponent was really fire and Thjalfi's was thought; the drinking horn Thor tried to empty was secretly connected to the sea, the cat was actually a segment of the Midgard Serpent, and the old woman was death.

Skuld

The NORN of the future. She was always veiled.

Sleipnir (= "the glider")

Odin's horse, sired on Loki by the stallion SVALDIFARI. It had eight legs and could outrun the wind, on water or land or through the air. Last seen at Ragnarok, where it impetuously carried its master down the gaping throat of the Fenris-wolf.

Sol

The Roman equivalent of the Greek Helios, the sun god.

Soma

An intoxicating liquor drunk, in Hindu mythology, by the Vedic priests. It was brought from the sky by an eagle and its consumption conferred eternal life.

[Aldous Huxley used the word in his *Brave New World* to describe the tranquillizer used to combat boredom in the monotonous Utopia of scientific paradise.]

Somnus

The Roman god of sleep, analogous to the Greek Hypnos. He was the son of Night and the brother of Death.

See THANATOS.

SPHINX

Sphinx

In Greek mythology the offspring of Echidna and Orthros, the Sphinx was a monster with the face (and often the breasts) of a woman, the body of a lion, and wings. Sent by Hera as an affliction on the city of Thebes, she guarded a narrow pass on a cliff by the sea and propounded to all who passed her famous riddle: What is it that in the morning walks on four legs, at noon on two, and in the evening on three? The answer—Man, who crawls as a baby, walks erect as a man, and leans on a staff in his old age—was given by OEDIPUS; whereupon the Sphinx hurled herself over the cliff to her death in the sea below.

Although the idea of the Sphinx was incorporated in Greek mythology from Egypt, the Egyptian Sphinx is quite different. There, a typification of the god Ra, it is a bearded man with a lion's body. The great Sphinx at Gizeh—perhaps the best known of all relics of antiquity—is far older than the Great Pyramid.

Starkadhr

A warrior in Norse mythology who continued to fight even after his head had been cut off.

[Starkadhr outdid even the redoubtable Witherington of the old ballad of *Chevy Chase,* who

> . . . when both his legs were hewn in two
> Yet he kneel'd and fought on his knee.

When Cardinal de Polignac told Madame du Deffand that Saint Denis after being decapitated had picked up his head and carried it two leagues on foot, that staunch old daughter of the Enlightenment replied, "But in such matters it is only the first step that is difficult."]

Stymphalian Birds

As one of his labors HERCULES was sent to rid the marshes of Stymphalus of a huge flock of monstrous birds. They had wings, beaks, and claws of iron, and lived exclusively on human flesh. He crouched under his impenetrable lion skin for protection and made such a racket banging on cymbals that the birds were frightened away and never returned.

Styx

1. Eldest daughter of Oceanus and Tethys. Mother of Zelus (zeal), Nike (victory), Kratos (power), and Bia (strength). In the war between the gods and the Titans she had aided Zeus. To honor her for this she was established as the supernatural being (though some include Themis) by whom the gods swore. If a god violated an oath which he had sworn by Styx he was compelled to remain speechless and breathless for a year and to be banished from the council of the gods for nine years.
2. The river of hate that wound five times around the underworld. Styx 1 was the nymph of this river. It is now the best known of the five rivers of hell—the one across which grim CHARON ferried the dead.

Suadela

The goddess of persuasion, attendant upon Aphrodite.

Svaldifari

The stallion of a disguised giant who offered, with the horse's help, to build the Norse gods an impregnable fortress. For wages he asked for the goddess Freya and the sun and the moon. Since the task—within the agreed time—seemed impossible the gods, at Loki's advice, accepted. Within a few days of the time limit, however, it became apparent that with the help of his incredible horse the stranger would finish the task and claim his reward. Loki disguised himself as a mare and distracted the stallion, so that the task was not completed. The "man" revealed himself to be a giant and Thor demolished him with his hammer.

Swanhild

Daughter of Sigurd and Gudrun in the *Volsung Saga*. She was so beautiful that wild horses refused to trample her to death until she was covered up.

Sword of Damocles

See DAMOCLES.

Symplegades

Rocks at the entrance to the Hellespont which clashed together when a ship tried to pass between them. Only one ship, indeed, had ever succeeded in passing between them. And that was the ARGO and she would have been crushed had not Hera, for love of Jason, given the Argonauts special protection. Iris, Hera's messenger, instructed them to make trial with a dove. The rocks rushed together as the dove darted through, but they only sheared off the bird's tail feathers. The Argonauts then rowed the *Argo* through with tremendous speed as the rocks were rebounding and managed to make it with the loss of only a part of the stern.

In the story of the Argonauts the rocks joined to become one fixed rock after the successful passage of the *Argo*. But if

—as seems likely—these were also the Planctae, the Wandering or Clashing Rocks mentioned in the *Odyssey,* there are at least two accounts of them. For even Zeus himself had no power over them. Every morning he sent two doves for his ambrosia; one was always crushed by the Clashing Rocks "and the Father has to add one more to maintain the tale."

[This would seem, at the worst, to be only a minor inconvenience to the Great Olympian. But it has a deeper significance. For it is one of the many little things in Greek mythology that show that the gods—even the Thunderer himself— are not omnipotent. On the periphery of their power, as it were, there are these slight abrasions, these faint menaces. If the gods swear by STYX, the oath is binding. There were powers before they were born. The hundred-handed ones still live and wait. The Titans are defeated but not annihilated. Though Aeschylus concludes the *Oresteia* by having the dreaded EUMENIDES, intimidated by Athena, consent to domestication, to being made subservient to human values, this is not their true nature; they are older than the upstart Olympians and, in some things, more powerful.

In Norse mythology this thought or feeling is much stronger. For the Norse gods are definitely doomed. Heimdal watches the Rainbow Bridge with ceaseless vigilance, but Ragnarok will come and gods and giants will be annihilated. With the assurance of another world, to be sure, but still *this* world and its gods will disappear.

In relation to mythology, this is good. It heightens tension and adds pathos. And it has an intellectual value, too; it suggests a profounder mystery than even religion can compass. It may be a weakness of Islam, Judaism, and Christianity that their god is omnipotent. Though there is always Judges 1:19 to brood over.]

SYRINX

Syrinx

A nymph who, fleeing from the god Pan, begged the river nymphs to help her. They changed her into a bed of reeds and from these Pan made the pipes that are always associated with him.

Talus

1. A bronze or iron mechanical man made by Hephaestus. He was the defender of Crete and kept enemies at bay by hurling huge rocks at them or, if they came near him, by heating himself red hot and embracing them. His vital fluids were vulnerable only in one foot and Medea killed him by cutting the membranes or pulling the brass nails of this foot. [His last literary appearance was in the company of Sir Artegal in Spenser's *Faerie Queene.*]

2. Also called *Perdix*. This Talus was the nephew of Daedalus, who slew him out of jealousy.

Tammuz (sometimes called **Thammuz** and **Adonis** [= "Lord"])

A Babylonian god of agriculture who annually died, descended into hell, and experienced a resurrection. His worship spread into Israel and "infected Sion's daughters" with "wanton passions" which Ezekiel saw when he "surveyed the dark idolatries of alienated Judah." Many things in his cult parallel Attis, Osiris, Adonis, Balder—and even more awesome figures.

TANTALUS

Tantalus

A son of Zeus, Tantalus was admitted to the company of the gods and, having eaten of their food, became immortal. However, he abused his privileges. There are various versions of his misdoings. One is that he stole ambrosia from the table of the gods and served it to mortals. Another is that he blabbed the table-talk of the gods. And still another that he invited the gods to dine with him and served them his own son PELOPS to test their omniscience. He was condemned to spend eternity in frustration: in Tartarus he stood in water up to his chin, but was wild with thirst because every time he tried to drink the water receded, and above his head were clusters of luscious fruits which the wind blew just beyond his reach whenever he tried to seize them.

[His name has given us the verb *tantalize*.]

Tarnkappe

The cap or cloak of invisibility by means of which Siegfried, in the *Nibelungenlied,* was able to win Brunhild for Gunther.

Tartarus

In Homer a region beneath Hades in which Zeus confined the defeated Titans. Later writers used the word as an equivalent of Hades. It was not necessarily a place of punishment, but some—Tantalus, Sisyphus—were punished there because they had offended the gods. They were not so much great offenders as offenders of the great.

See SALMONEUS.

Telamon

The brother of PELEUS and the father of AJAX and the archer TEUCER.

Telegonus

Son of ODYSSEUS and CIRCE (on whom Odysseus also begot Agrius and Latinus). Circe, after some years, sent Telegonus in search of his father. He landed on Ithaca, not knowing what island it was, and while plundering was attacked by Odysseus. In the fight Odysseus was killed by the spear which Circe had given their son. Telegonus later married PENELOPE, and Telemachus, Odysseus' son by Penelope, married Circe.

[As complicated a happy ending as soap opera ever saw in its most iridescent bubbles!]

Telemachus

Son of Odysseus and Penelope. In the *Odyssey* he seeks news of his father from Nestor and from Menelaus, and returns to Ithaca in time to help his father slay the suitors. In some versions of his story he marries Circe after his father's death.

Telephus

King of the Mysians. A son of Hercules, he was wounded by Achilles when the Greeks on their way to Troy landed on Mysia. The wound proved incurable. The oracle at Delphi said, "He that wounded shall also heal" and so Telephus set out to find Achilles. Scrapings from Achilles' spear were applied to the wound and healed it.

Tellus

The ancient Roman earth goddess, equivalent to the Greek Gaea.

Tentagil (modern **Tintagel**)

The castle, in Malory's *Morte d'Arthur,* wherein Uther Pendragon begot Arthur on Lady Igraine.

Tereus

See PHILOMELA.

Terpsichore

Muse of the dance and lyric poetry.

Terra

The Roman goddess analogous to the Greek GAEA or GE.

Tethys

Daughter of Uranus and Gaea, the wife and sister of Oceanus, to whom she bore the rivers and the three thousand Oceanides.

Teucer

The son of Telamon and Hesione. One of the more distinguished warriors on the Grecian side in the Trojan War, he was an archer and loosed his shafts from behind the mighty shield of his gigantic half brother, the Telamonian Ajax. On returning home, after Ajax had committed suicide, he was banished by his angry and grief-stricken father.

Teuthras

King of Mysia. Hunting in the mountains he roused a huge boar which fled to the temple of Artemis, crying "Spare me, I belong to the goddess." Teuthras killed the boar, nonetheless, which so offended the goddess that she gave him leprosy. His mother, Leucippe, appeased the goddess with many gifts, among which was a golden mechanical boar, with a man's head, which repeated the words "Spare me!" The goddess was particularly pleased with this and cured Teuthras' leprosy.

Thalia

1. The Muse of comedy.
2. One of the GRACES.
3. A Nereid.

Thamyris (or Thamyras)

A musician of Thrace who presumptuously boasted he was a better musician than the Muses. Apollo (who was a rival to Thamyris for the love of Hyacinthus—for Thamyris was claimed by some to be the first mortal pederast) maliciously repeated the boast to the Muses. They deprived the wretched Thamyris of his sight and his voice and broke his lyre.

Thanatos

In Greek mythology, death personified. He was the son of Night and the brother of Sleep and even the gods hated him. He often came after the dead and it was from him that Hercules wrested ALCESTIS.

Thaumas

Son of Pontus and Gaea and father, by the Oceanid Electra, of the HARPIES and of IRIS.

Thebes

The capital of Boeotia. Founded by Cadmus. Ruled over by LAIUS, OEDIPUS, and CREON. Successfully resisted the Seven who came against her but was destroyed by the sons of the Seven, the EPIGONI.

See OEDIPUS, SEVEN AGAINST THEBES, ANTIGONE.

Themis

Daughter of Uranus and Gaea, she was the goddess of order and justice, mother of the seasons and the Fates. The gods bound their solemn oaths in her name (as also that of Styx).

Theoclymenus

The fugitive seer whom Telemachus takes on board his ship as he leaves Pylos to return to Ithaca. He encourages Telemachus by his interpretation of an omen.

Thersites

A foul-mouthed common soldier in the Grecian army—the only common soldier mentioned in the *Iliad*. He taunted Agamemnon and was beaten by Odysseus. When, however, he scurrilously taunted Achilles for mourning over the dead Penthesilea (queen of the Amazons who fought for the Trojans and was eventually killed by Achilles) Achilles killed him. This caused a quarrel between Achilles and Diomedes, whose kinsman Thersites was.

Theseus

Chief mythological hero of Athens. Son of Aegeus, king of Athens, and his queen, Aethra.

Among his feats were the slaying of Periphetes, the savage and gigantic son of Hephaestus, and the slaying of PROCRUSTES. He was one of the Argonauts. At Athens his stepmother, the witch Medea, tried to poison him. But his father recognized him as his son (by the sword he bore) and Medea fled. Declared successor to the throne, he freed Athens from the tribute of youths and maidens which King MINOS compelled them to send each year to Crete—to be devoured by the Minotaur. In this adventure he was assisted by ARIADNE, daughter of Minos, whom he abandoned on the island of Naxos. He had promised his father that if he was successful and slew the Minotaur he would herald the event by hoisting white sails—instead of the customary black sails—on the vessel he would return in. But he forgot to do this and Aegeus, thinking his son dead, threw himself into the sea from a high cliff and was drowned.

As king of Athens, Theseus overcame the Amazons and carried off their queen, ANTIOPE, reclaimed the Marathonian bull, assisted his friend Pirithous (*see* LAPITHAE) in his battle with the Centaurs, and went with him down into Hades to help him abduct Persephone. In this they were unsuccessful and Theseus escaped only by the aid of Hercules.

After Antiope's death Theseus married Phaedra, sister of the Ariadne he had deserted earlier. She became enamoured of his son Hippolytus (child of either Antiope or her sister Hippolyte) and when her advances were rejected she accused him of attempting to violate her. Theseus begged Poseidon to kill the young man—who was dragged to death behind his chariot when Poseidon sent a bull which, rising from the sea, frightened Hippolytus' horses.

In his old age Theseus gave up the kingship of Athens and retired to Scyros, where he was treacherously murdered by King Lycomedes.

Thetis

A Nereid, wife of Peleus and mother of ACHILLES. It was decreed by Fate that she should bear a son who would be mightier than his father. Zeus and Poseidon both desired her, ignorant of the doom implicit in a union with her—a doom

THISBE

the possibility of which would cause great alarm in a family in which the son had twice been mightier than the father and had destroyed the father (Zeus/Cronus, Cronus/Uranus). However, when informed by Themis, the gods gave her to PELEUS and it was at their wedding that Eris, the goddess of discord, flung down the famous golden apple. Some versions of the legend say that Themis informed the gods directly of their danger; others have it that she gave the information to PROMETHEUS as something by the divulging of which he could obtain his freedom.

Thisbe

See PYRAMUS AND THISBE.

Thoas

King of the Lemnians who, at the general massacre of all the men of his kingdom by their resentful wives *(see* LEMNOS), was secretly spared by his daughter, HYPSIPYLE, who set him adrift in an oarless boat. Thoas was driven ashore on the island of Sicinos and lived to reign over the Taurians.

Thokk

The malicious old woman who, alone in the entire world, refused to weep for Balder dead and so prevented his returning to life. Actually she was Loki in disguise.

Thor

The god of thunder in Norse mythology. He was the son of Odin. But though he was perpetually at war with the giants, he was, in many ways—his roughness, his grossness, his huge appetite—more like one of the giants than like one of the gods. He is famed for his hammer (the thunderbolt), which always returned to his hand after being hurled, for the belt which gave him ever-renewed power, and for the iron gloves that made him invincible. His house was Bilskinir.

Thoth

The Egyptian god of learning, inventor of writing, arithmetic, astronomy. He settled disputes among the gods. He is represented as with the head of an ibis or of a baboon. He knew the secrets that the dead had to know to pass into the underworld, and for this, and other reasons, the Greeks identified him with Hermes.

Thrym

King of the Frost Giants in Norse mythology. He stole and buried Thor's hammer and demanded the goddess Freya as the price of its restoration. Thor dressed as Freya and when the hammer was laid in his lap, as a wedding gift, slew Thrym.

Thyestes

Son of Pelops and Hippodameia and the brother of ATREUS. Thyestes seduced his brother's wife, Aerope, and Atreus sought revenge by killing Thyestes' sons and serving them as meat to their unsuspecting father. The blood feud continued until Thyestes' son Aegisthus (product of an incestuous union between Thyestes and his daughter Pelopia) seduced Clytemnestra, the wife of Atreus' son Agamemnon, and assisted in the murder of Agamemnon. Aegisthus was then killed by Agamemnon's son Orestes. Athena finally put an end to this bloody series by purifying Orestes.

TIAMAT

Tiamat

The primeval dragon in Babylonian mythology, the great bottomless sea whence all things came. She was slain by Marduk and from her corpse heaven and earth were fashioned.

Tiresias

The blind Theban seer, most famous of seers in Greek mythology. There are two accounts of his blindness:

(1) As a child he accidentally came upon Athena in her bath and she splashed water in his eyes. In recompense, at the beseeching of his mother, the goddess gave him the power of prophecy, the ability to understand the speech of birds, and a staff that enabled him to walk as safely as if he had his sight.

(2) He had at one time been changed to a woman and then, later, back to a man again. So that he alone, of all living things, knew the experience of both sexes. For this reason he was called on to settle an argument between Zeus and Hera on the comparative pleasure that men or women enjoyed in coition. He said that women had nine times more pleasure than men—an answer which aroused the hostility of Hera, who blinded him. Zeus, however, to make amends, gave him the power of prophecy; but Hera, who could not take away the gift, modified it by saying that no one would believe his prophecies (*see* CASSANDRA).

It was to get advice from Tiresias that Odysseus went down into the underworld. It was upon Tiresias that Oedipus called to find the reason for the plague that was decimating Thebes.

[It was because of his wisdom and his unique knowledge of

love that T. S. Eliot made him the figure, in *The Waste Land,* whose vision "is the substance of the poem."]

Tisiphone

One of the EUMENIDES.

Titans

In Greek mythology the old gods (children of Uranus and Gaea) who ruled before the Olympian gods. They are usually listed as twelve, though Hesiod lists thirteen and Homer speaks of only two. The twelve are six males (Oceanus, Coeus, Crius, Hyperion, Iapetus, and Cronus) and six females (Thea, Rhea, Themis, Mnemosyne, Phoebe, and Tethys). They were imprisoned by their father, Uranus, but Cronus overthrew him and castrated him. CRONUS was in his turn defeated (and bound down in Tartarus) by his son Zeus, but not without a terrible and prolonged war in which the Olympians finally achieved victory only with the help of the Hecatoncheires *(see* BRIAREUS).

Tithonus

See EOS.

Tityus

A giant, one of the sons of Gaea, whom Odysseus saw when he visited Hades. He was so huge that his recumbent form covered nine acres. He was chained and two vultures tore ceaselessly at his liver as punishment for his having attacked Leto.

Tjasse

A storm giant in Norse mythology. The goddess Idunn, keeper of the apples of youth which eternally rejuvenated the gods, was betrayed into Tjasse's power by Loki. In her absence the gods began to grow old and Loki was compelled to go to Tjasse's hall and bring her back. He managed to do it, with the aid of magic, but at great risk, almost the loss of his life. In the return flight Tjasse was killed.

Tor

A knight of King Arthur's Round Table, bastard son of King Pellanor and a milkmaid.

Triptolemus

See CELEUS.

Tristram

In Malory's *Morte d'Arthur,* the son of Meliodas, king of Lyonesse, and Elizabeth, sister of King Mark of Cornwall. Sent to Ireland to be cured of a wound, he falls in love with La Beale Isoud and she returns his love. He is later sent back to Ireland to ask for the hand of Isoud for King Mark. The request is granted by her parents and Mark and Isoud are married. Tristram leaves Mark's court and, fighting in Brittany, falls in love with Isoud la Blanche Mains (= "Isolde of the White Hands"). However, he returns to Cornwall and is slain by King Mark.

Another account has it that, wounded by a poisoned arrow, Tristram sends for Isoud of Ireland. If she comes, the ship is to have white sails; if not, black. Isoud la Blanche Mains knows of this arrangement and as the ship approaches lies and tells the sick man that its sails are black. He lies in despair and Isoud of Ireland, finding him dead, dies also.

[The story is treated in Matthew Arnold's *Tristram and Iseult,* in Swinburne's *Tristram of Lyonesse,* and in Richard Wagner's *Tristan und Isolde.* Lyonesse is supposed to be a tract of land—now submerged—between the southwestern tip of Cornwall and the Scilly Islands.]

Triton(s)

There was a gigantic sea god, Triton, son of Poseidon and Amphitrite, who lived at the bottom of the sea. But by later Greek mythology his name had been applied to a class of minor sea gods, men from the waist up and fish from the waist down. They are commonly represented as blowing on a conch shell ("or hear old Triton blow his wreatèd horn"). Vergil recounts that the trumpeter Misenus (after whom Cape Misenum in the Bay of Naples is named) was drowned by an indignant Triton whom he had challenged to a contest of musical skill.

Trivia

One of the Roman names for Diana, the Roman equivalent of the Greek Artemis and sometimes Hecate. She was so called because, like Hecate, she was worshipped at a crossroads.

Troilus

The *Iliad* merely mentions Troilus ("the chariot-warrior") as one of the slain sons for whom Priam laments. Vergil, in the *Aeneid,* states that he was killed by Achilles. The story of Troilus and Cressida was developed in the Middle Ages and has no basis in Greek mythology.

Trojan Horse (or Wooden Horse)

A huge wooden horse, made by Epeius (upon the suggestion of Athena), within whose hollow belly were concealed some Grecian warriors. Deceived by various ruses, the Trojans dragged the horse through their otherwise impregnable walls, deeming it to be an offering to Athena. At night those hidden in the horse emerged and opened the gates to their waiting comrades, who seized and sacked the city.

Trojan War

A war waged for ten years by the Achaeans (Greeks), under the command of Agamemnon, to recover Helen, wife of Menelaus (Agamemnon's brother), who had been abducted by Paris, son of Priam, the king of Troy. The first nine years were taken up by a siege, enlivened by various individual combats. The events of the tenth year are related in the *Iliad.* Other, later, accounts speak of the involvement of the Amazons and the Ethiopians. Troy was finally taken by the ruse of the Wooden Horse, and the city was burned and its inhabitants either put to the sword or taken into captivity. Subsequent events concerning some of the principal figures are related in the *Odyssey* and various of the Greek plays, especially the trilogy that constitutes the *Oresteia* of Aeschylus.

See: ACHILLES, AGAMEMNON, AJAX, ARES, ASTYANAX, BRISEIS, CLYTEMNESTRA, DIOMEDES, ERIS, GLAUCUS, HECTOR, HECUBA, HELEN, ILIAD, IPHIGENIA, MENELAUS, NEOPTOLEMUS, ODYSSEUS, PARIS, PENTHESILEA, PHILOCTETES, PRIAM, THERSITES, THETIS, et al.

Trolls

The trolls are uncertain, shadowy figures in Scandinavian mythology. They were originally Jotuns, but strange creatures even for Jotuns—some of them having as many as fifty heads. Sometimes they were thought of as dwarfs. They lived (or live) in caves and underground and burst if sunlight touches them.

They are mischievous and malicious and, for the most part, un- and anti-human. They are not Christian devils, for these

—for all their evil—are a part of God's world. But the trolls, like the Jotuns, are outside of a man-centered or god-centered world.

They guard treasures and can do a man a good turn if they want to. But the man who has to do with them may come to a bad end, for they are capricious and in accepting their aid a man sets himself apart from humanity and humaneness.

[Halvard Solness, Ibsen's Master Builder, believes he owes some of his success to the trolls. But he is aware that to feed his vitality they have drawn the lifeblood out of his wife Aline and hence loaded him with guilt. Then he suspects there is a troll in Hilda Wangel—the young girl who so strongly excites his aging masculinity—and, as he may have perceived in the last few seconds of his consciousness, drives him to his death.]

Trophonius

Architect and brother of Agamedes. They built the temple of Apollo at Delphi. Caught in the act of stealing treasure (while building a treasury), Trophonius cut off his brother's head—so that there could be no witness against him. For this dreadful act he was swallowed by the earth and became a cave oracle at Lebadea. As an oracle he generally took the darker, realistic view, and it was well known that those who consulted him were usually depressed by his predictions.

Turnus

King of the Rutulians who, in the *Aeneid*, fought Aeneas for LAVINIA and was killed.

Twelve Labors of Hercules

See HERCULES.

Tyche (Roman **Fortuna**)

The Greek goddess who personified good fortune. She was sometimes regarded as a fourth Fate, but not legitimately so. She was commonly represented with the cornucopia of abundance and the wheel of chance.

Tydeus

Son of Oeneus and father of Diomedes. He joined the Seven in their expedition against Thebes. For the story of his death, *see* MELANIPPUS.

Tyndareus

The husband of Leda and the father—or assumed father—of HELEN, CLYTEMNESTRA, CASTOR AND POLLUX.

Typhon (also **Typhoeus**)

A huge monster who fought with Zeus, was defeated and buried under Mount Aetna, whose volcanic rumblings and eruptions are the monster's struggles.

Tyr (or **Tiu**—after whom Tuesday is named)

The Norse god of war, a son of Odin. He had only one hand, the other having been bitten off by the wolf Fenrir, who demanded that Tyr place his hand in Fenrir's mouth when the gods bound the wolf (in pretended playfulness) with the magic thread GLEIPNIR. At Ragnarok, Tyr will kill and be killed by Garm, the hound of Hel.

Tyro

A nymph, wife of Crethus, to whom she bore Aeson, Pheres, and Amathaon. She was loved by the river god Enipeus. Poseidon assumed the form of Enipeus and begot PELIAS and NELEUS on her.

Ull

The Norse god of skiers, son of Sif.

[The d'Aulaires *(Norse Gods,* New York, 1967) believe Ull to have been a very ancient god. Judging from the number of Scandinavian place names that incorporate his name, they believe that he must, at one time, have been a very important god. But memory of him had almost faded away by the time the *Eddas* were composed.]

Ulysses

The Latin name for ODYSSEUS.

Urania

The Muse of astronomy.

[Milton invokes her aid in the opening lines of the seventh book of *Paradise Lost.* It is she who, with sublime egotism, he begs to find for his poem "fit audience, though few."]

Uranus

The sky. Son and husband of Gaea, the earth, and father by her of the Titans, the Cyclops, and the hundred-handed monsters (Hecatoncheires). He confined his progeny in TARTARUS and this angered Gaea, who supported her son Cronus in his revolt against his father. Cronus overcame and castrated

Uranus and chained him down in Tartarus. From the blood of the mutilated Uranus sprang the Eumenides and the giants.

Urd

The NORN of the past, the oldest of the three. She is always looking back.

Utgard-Loki

See SKRYMIR.

Uther Pendragon

King of England at some primitive, dateless time. Father by Igraine, wife of Duke Gorlois of Cornwall, of King Arthur. The union was arranged by the wizard Merlin, to whom the rearing of the child was entrusted. After the death of Gorlois, Uther married Igraine.

Valhalla

The great hall of the castle of Gladsheim, in Asgärd. It was so huge that it had five hundred and forty doors, through each of which eight hundred men could march abreast. It was the feasting hall of the Einherjar, the heroes who had been selected, because of their prowess on the field of battle, by the Valkyries and brought to Valhalla to fight and die once again at Ragnarok. Every night they feasted and caroused and every day—to keep in trim—they hacked and hewed each other in battle, being miraculously restored to wholeness at the end of each day's carnage.

[These daily fights would have been no fun, of course, had not the heroes been in true, warlike fury. And to achieve this heroic state they ate certain toadstools! The knowledge of these "mind-expanding" drugs is, plainly, very old, even in Europe.]

Vali

Youngest of Odin's sons, one of the seven Aesir to survive Ragnarok.

Valkyries

Priestesses of Freya, in Norse mythology. Attended by Skuld, the Norn of the future, they rode aerial horses into battle, selected those heroes destined to be slain and bore them after death to Valhalla, where they waited on them at their feasting. Chief among them were Mista, Sangrida, and Hilda.

Vampires

Evil spirits—sometimes assumed to be the souls of heretics —that, in Slavic mythology and folklore, assume the form of bats and at night suck the blood of the living as they lie asleep. The victim often becomes a vampire himself.

Vanir

Gods, in Norse mythology, older than the Aesir—with whom in time they were syncretized. They were originally rain gods. They lived in Vanaheim.

Venus

An obscure Italian goddess of beauty and charm who by the third century B.C. had become identified with the Greek Aphrodite.

[Like Hercules, Mars, Mercury, Vulcan, Juno, and some others, the Latin name is now the more common, at least in English usage. The Greek attributes of the deity are largely retained, however.]

Verdandi

The Norn of the present.
See NORNS.

Vertumnus

Roman god of the seasons, husband of the goddess of fruits, Pomona.

VESTA

Vesta

The Roman hearth goddess. Her name is etymologically the same as the Greek *Hestia*. She was worshipped in every house and by an eternal flame in a special building. The flame was tended by six Vestal Virgins who, selected at the age of six to ensure their virginity, served for a minimum of five years. If at any time during their tenure of office they lost their virginity, they were buried alive.

Victoria

The Roman goddess of victory, analogous to the Greek NIKE.

Vidar

The son of Odin, in Norse mythology. One of the strongest of the gods. At Ragnarok, after Fenris-wolf has killed his father, he will tear the wolf in pieces.

Vigrid

The battlefield of Ragnarok. It was one hundred miles square.

[At the time of the *Eddas* a battle area of this size was as wild and poetic a concept as hundred-headed trolls or eight-legged horses. But, alas, in this, as in so much else, we have outdone the imagination of the past, and for the worse. A modern generalissimo could hardly wish for anything better than for his enemy to be lured into so restricted and tidy an area—where two or three hydrogen bombs would settle the matter between sunup and breakfast.]

Vivien

The name in "Merlin and Vivien," in Tennyson's *Idylls of the King,* of the wily young woman who wheedles from Merlin a magic charm by which she imprisons him. In Malory's *Morte d'Arthur* her name is given as NINEVE, *Nimue,* or *Nimiane.*

Volsung Saga

Volsung, great-grandson of Odin, ruled the Huns. He had ten sons, of whom Sigmund, the eldest, was the most valiant. And he had one daughter, Signy, who was sought in marriage by Siggeir, king of the Goths. They are married and at the wedding a mysterious stranger (Odin in disguise) thrusts a sword into the trunk of a tree and states that it will confer irresistible prowess on whoever is able to pluck it out. All try, but only Sigmund succeeds. Siggeir is jealous and by treachery slays Volsung and all the sons except Sigmund, who is saved by his sister Signy—upon whom, through her wiles, he has unwittingly begotten a heroic son, Sinfiotli. For a while father and son are outlaws and even werewolves. They finally burn Siggeir and his children and Signy dies in the fire.

Sinfiotli is poisoned by Sigmund's wife Borghild and soon after this she dies. Sigmund then marries Hiordis. But soon after this second marriage he is killed, leaving Hiordis pregnant. To her is born his posthumous son, Sigurd, the greatest of the Volsungs. He is reared by Regin, a blacksmith, who teaches him runes and other wisdom. He tells him, among other things, of the magic ring of Andvari and the ill-gotten gold hoard brooded over by Fafnir in the form of a dragon. Sigurd slays Fafnir and, by eating his heart, learns the language of birds. He takes the gold and the ring and comes to the hill of Hindfell, where, inside a wall of fire, he finds asleep in a castle the warrior maiden Brunhild (actually a Valkyrie, whom her father Odin has put into an enchanted sleep). Sigurd awakens her; they love and plight their troth, he giving her the ring of Andvari.

VOLVA

Subsequently, however, Sigurd, visiting the court of the Nibelungs, is given a magic potion by Grimhild, the mother of Gudrun, which erases all memory of Brunhild and leads him to marry Gudrun. Gunnar, Gudrun's brother, desires to marry Brunhild and Sigurd, assuming Gunnar's semblance, rides again through the flames of Hindfell, this time to win Brunhild for Gunnar. She accepts and gives him the ring of Andvari. At the wedding, however, Sigurd recognizes her, Grimhild's magic potion having lost its effect. Sigurd gives the ring to Gudrun.

Brunhild and Gudrun quarrel and Gudrun taunts Brunhild and shows her the fatal ring. Brunhild incites Guttorm, Gudrun's brother, to murder Sigurd and at his death Brunhild kills herself and is burned beside Sigurd on his funeral pyre. Gudrun then marries Atli, king of the Huns, who desires the gold hoard (which is concealed at the bottom of the Rhine) and, when he can't get it, treacherously kills her brothers. Gudrun then slays him and sets fire to his hall.

Taking her beautiful daughter by Sigurd, Swanhild, Gudrun goes to the realm of King Jonakr, who becomes her third husband. Swanhild is murdered by Jormunrek—who has her trampled to death by wild horses (though it is necessary to cover her first; her beauty is so great that the horses cannot bring themselves to trample her while they can see her). Gudrun sends her sons by Jonakr to avenge Swanhild's death. They slay Jormunrek but are themselves killed in the action.

Gudrun calls on Sigurd to return from the dead and look on her once more as she lies dying.

Volva

In Norse mythology a wise woman, long dead, who could be compelled by magic to come back to life and prophesy—as the woman of Endor (I Samuel 28) could, apparently, compel the spirit of Samuel to arise from the dead and prophesy to Saul.

In the poetic *Edda* a Volva revealed past, present, and future to Odin. A nice eerie, poetic touch is added by her continually asking him, as she described the various horrors of things to come, "Do you know more now, or not?"

Vulcan

The Roman god corresponding to the Greek Hephaestus. Vulcan, originally simply a god of fire, became, under the syncretizing influence of Hephaestus, an artificer. His assistants were the Cyclops. They had their smithies underground and the heat and sparks from these belched forth from volcanoes. The god's own forge was thought to be below Aetna.

Wandering Rocks

See SYMPLEGADES.

Werewolf

In Teutonic and Slavic mythology, one capable of turning himself into a wolf. The first element is probably an Indo-European word for *man* (cf. Latin *vir*). A more learned word for becoming a wolf or for imagining that one is a wolf is *lycanthropy*.

Wooden Horse

See TROJAN HORSE.

Wotan (also **Woden**)

The West Germanic form of ODIN. It is the first part of our word *Wednesday*.

Xanthus

1. The name of the god of the river Scamander, which flowed past Troy.
2. A river in Lycia, sacred to Apollo.
3. One of the horses of Achilles, sired by Podarge (either one of the Harpies or one of Hector's horses). In a curious passage in the *Iliad* Xanthus, suddenly endowed with the power of speech by the goddess Hera, rebukes Achilles for upbraiding his horses (Xanthus and Balius) for allowing Patroclus to be killed by Hector. But the Eumenides "stayed his voice." For even though the consort of Zeus herself had given the horse the power of speech, such a thing was contrary to the order of nature and hence its correction was within the province of the Eumenides. Xanthus prophesied Achilles' own death and Achilles answered, in effect, "Yes, I know, I know; *you* don't have to tell me!"

Xuthus

The second son of Hellen, who was the son of Deucalion. He married Creusa, a daughter of Erechtheus. She had previously borne a son Ion to Apollo, but the child was taken from her at its birth. She and Xuthus were childless and consulted the oracle at Delphi, which counselled them to adopt as their son the first young man they met. And this happened to be Ion, who had been brought up in the temple of Apollo at Delphi.

Ygg (= "the terrible one")

Odin's name when considered as the god of storm and war.

Yggdrasil

The world tree (an ash) that, in Norse mythology, binds heaven, earth, and hell together. It is fed by three mystic springs. Its branches reach heaven and spread over earth. At its roots lie magic runes. At its top sits an eagle and gnawing at its roots crouches the dragon Nidhug. And between them, seeking to stir up trouble, runs the squirrel Ratatösk.

Ymir

The first of the giants in Norse mythology and the begetter of the entire race. He was killed by Odin, Vili, and Ve, who built the universe from his carcass.

Yule

A Norse festival in which sacrifices were made to the Aesir. It was held, at various periods, anywhere from mid-November to mid-January, but gradually became identified with Christmas and other festivities that joyfully greeted the returning sun at the winter solstice.

Zelus

Son of the Titan Pallas (not to be confused with Pallas Athena) and the river Styx. The name means "zeal."

Zephyrus (or Favonius)

The West Wind. Was in love with Chloris, the goddess of spring (Latin *Flora),* though sometimes represented as married to Iris, goddess of the rainbow and messenger of the gods. In some versions he is the father of Achilles' famous horses, Xanthus and Balius, by the Harpy Podarge (="shining foot").

[That mares could be impregnated by the wind was a widespread belief.]

Zethus

See Amphion, Dirce.

Zeus

The supreme deity in Greek mythology, Zeus was the son of the Titans Cronus and Rhea. Reared in a secret cave on Mount Ida and suckled by a she-goat, when he reached maturity he overthrew his father and established the rule of the Olympian gods (so called from their living on the top of Mount Olympus). Originally, apparently, he was a rain god, the god of the sky, of the thunder and the thunderbolt. He is represented as a stern but benign figure, as a bearded man in full physical maturity.

As the All-Father, the Greeks had to make Zeus polygamous or promiscuous (as Graves has said) and chose the latter as being less offensive to their mores. By his sister and wife Hera he sired Ares, Hephaestus, Hebe, and Eileithyia. Athena he literally "made up out of his own head." By various goddesses and mortal women he was the father of Apollo, Artemis, the Horae and the Moerae, Hermes, Aphrodite, Dionysus, Persephone, Hercules, Perseus, Helen, and many others.

GREEK AND ROMAN NAMES

The Romans adopted a great deal of Greek mythology and adapted many of their legends and names to make them correspond to their Greek equivalents. *Hercules* is, obviously, simply a variant spelling of the Greek *Heracles,* as is the Latin *Vesta* of the Greek *Hestia.* Others are more deeply hidden—as, for instance (as assumed by many scholars), the name *Zeus* in the first syllable of *Jupiter.* But many are clearly totally different words—as the Latin *Vulcan* and the Greek *Hephaestus*—and it is probable that they originally designated wholly unrelated deities. Here is a partial list of parallel gods and heroes. That the Latin names are better known reflects the wider use of Latin in western Europe during the first fifteen to eighteen centuries of our era.

Greek	Latin
Aphrodite	Venus
Apollo	Phoebus
Ares	Mars
Artemis	Diana
Athena	Minerva
Cronus	Saturn
Demeter	Ceres

Dionysus	Bacchus
Eileithyia	Lucina
Eos	Aurora
Erinyes	Furies
Eris	Discordia
Eros	Cupid
Gaea	Tellus
Hades	Dis, Pluto, Plutus, Orcus
Hebe	Juventas
Hecate	Trivia
Hephaestus	Vulcan
Hera	Juno
Heracles	Hercules
Hermes	Mercury
Hestia	Vesta
Hypnos	Somnus
Leto	Latona
Moerae	Parcae
Nike	Victoria
Odysseus	Ulysses
Pan	Inuus, Faunus
Persephone	Proserpina
Pluto	Dis
Poseidon	Neptune
Rhea	Ops
Selene	Diana
Tyche	Fortuna
Zeus	Jupiter

SELECTED BIBLIOGRAPHY

BELLAMY, H. S. *Moons, Myths and Man.* London, 1949.

BRANSTON, B. *The Gods of the North.* New York, n.d.

BRAY, O. (trans.). *The Elder Edda.* London, 1908.

Brewer's Dictionary of Phrase and Fable. London, 1963 (8th ed.).

Bulfinch's Mythology. New York, 1934.

CARPENTER, R. *Folk-tale, Fiction, and Saga in the Homeric Epic.* Berkeley, 1956.

COLUM, PADRAIC. *The Golden Fleece.* New York, 1921.

CRAIGIE, SIR WILLIAM A. *The Icelandic Sagas.* Cambridge, 1913.

————. *The Religion of Ancient Scandinavia.* London, 1914.

D'AULAIRE, INGRI, and EDGAR PARIN. *Norse Gods and Giants.* New York, 1967.

FAIRBANKS, H. *The Mythology of Greece and Rome.* New York, 1907.

FARADAY, W. *Divine Mythology of the North.* London, 1902.

FORSDYKE, J. *Greece Before Homer.* New York, 1964.

FRAZER, SIR JAMES G. *The Golden Bough.* 12 vols. London, 1911–15.

GAYLEY, CHARLES M. *The Classic Myths.* New York, 1911.

GRAVES, ROBERT. *The Greek Myths.* 2 vols. Baltimore, 1955.

SELECTED BIBLIOGRAPHY

GRIMM, J. *Teutonic Mythology*. Trans. T. S. STALYBRASS. London, 1880.

HAMILTON, EDITH. *Mythology*. New York, 1942.

HARVEY, SIR PAUL (ed.). *Oxford Companion to Classical Literature*. Oxford, 1951.

Hastings Encyclopaedia of Religion and Ethics. 13 vols. New York, 1908–27.

HAZLITT, WILLIAM CAREW. *Dictionary of Faiths and Folklore*. London, 1905.

LANG, ANDREW. *Customs and Myth*. London, 1901.

MUNDI, P. *Norse Mythology*. New York, 1926.

MURRAY, ALEXANDER S. *Manual of Mythology*. New York, 1935.

MURRAY, SIR GILBERT. *Five Stages of Greek Religion*. Oxford, 1925.

NILSSON, M. P. *A History of Greek Religion*. Trans. F. J. FIELDEN. Oxford, 1925.

OTTO, W. *The Homeric Gods*. London, 1964.

Oxford Classical Dictionary. Oxford, 1961.

RHYS, JOHN. *The Arthurian Legend*. Oxford, 1891.

ROSE, H. J. *A Handbook of Greek Mythology*. New York, 1950.

SCUDDER, VIDA D. *Le Morte Darthur of Sir Thomas Malory*. London & New York, 1917.

SEYFFERT, OSKAR. *A Dictionary of Classical Antiquities*. Revised, HENRY NETTLESHIP and J. E. SANDYS. New York, 1956.

SPENCE, L. *Introduction to Mythology*. London, 1931.

Standard Dictionary of Folklore. Ed. MARIA LEACH. 2 vols. New York, 1949.

INDEX

NOTE: Index main entries that occur in the *Dictionary* as separate entries appear in small caps. Regular type is used for names that do not occur as a separate entry in the *Dictionary*. Index references are to main entries, so that all available information can quickly be found.

INDEX

INDEX

INDEX

INDEX

INDEX

INDEX

INDEX

INDEX

INDEX

INDEX

INDEX

INDEX

INDEX

INDEX